W9-BFM-387

who   what   where

when   how

FLASH
FORWARD
READING

fact   opinion

Written by **Kathryn O'Dell**

Illustrations by **David Coulson**

Flash Kids™
Spark Publishing

Spark Publishing
A Division of Barnes & Noble
120 Fifth Avenue
New York, NY 10011
www.sparknotes.com

ISBN-13: 978-1-4114-0707-7
ISBN-10: 1-4114-0707-5

For more information, please visit *www.flashkidsbooks.com*
Please submit changes or report errors to *www.flashkidsbooks.com/errors*

Printed and bound in the United States

1 3 5 7 9 10 8 6 4 2

Dear Parent,

As your child encounters higher levels of reading difficulty, it is vital that he or she not only follows along with the text, but also understands the meaning of what is being read. Comprehension is often very difficult for young readers, but practice is proven to develop it. Here to help your child with reading comprehension skills are almost 100 pages of questions that accompany short stories and other passages of interest to fifth-graders.

This colorful workbook features entertaining readings followed by activities that will help your child focus on key skills such as: identifying the main idea and supporting details; vocabulary building; and differentiating between fact, opinion, and inference. He or she will practice a range of test-taking formats, too—from multiple-choice and sequencing to short answer questions.

The activities are designed for your child to handle alone, but you can read along and help with any troublesome words, ideas, or questions. Patience is key for reading comprehension. Then together you can check answers at the back of the workbook, and you should always give praise and encouragement for his or her effort. In addition, try to find other ways for your child to practice reading comprehension. You can pick out a newspaper article for your child to read. Ask your child to summarize the article and identify the main idea. Remember that reading is everywhere, so just use your imagination!

Space Station Living

Have you ever thought about living in outer space? Some astronauts live in space on space stations for weeks, months, or even years. The biggest space station is the International Space Station (ISS).

Many countries are working together to build ISS. These countries include the United States, Russia, Japan, Canada, Brazil, and many countries in Europe. Astronauts work in crews that live on the space station. ISS has room for three people to be there at a time. The first crew to live on ISS moved there in 2000. ISS is supposed to be finished in 2010. When it's done, it will weigh more than 1 million pounds.

ISS is about 250 miles above earth. It travels at about 17,200 miles per hour. It orbits earth, and it takes about $1\frac{1}{2}$ hours for it to go around earth. ISS gets its energy from the sun. It has many solar panels on it.

Astronauts go up in space in a space shuttle to get to ISS. When they are there, they live inside the space station. Since there isn't any gravity in space, they float around in the space station. They hook sleeping bags to a wall at night, so they can sleep without floating around. There isn't a washing machine on the space station, so astronauts wear disposable clothes. They wear them for three days, and then they throw them away. There is a shower on the space station, but astronauts have to conserve water.

Astronauts eat food three times a day on the space station. They have to be careful or the food will float away! This is not only messy, but it can be dangerous if the food gets into the expensive equipment. They eat soup and soda in plastic bags through a straw. They eat bigger meals at tables. The knives, forks, and spoons connect to the table with magnets so they don't float away during meals.

When they leave the space station to work on the outside of it, they must put on space suits. Astronauts are busy on the space station fixing it, building it, and doing research. When they have a few free minutes, they might send e-mails back to earth or watch DVDs!

Read each question. Circle the correct answer.

1. What does ISS stand for?
   a. International Stations in Space
   b. International Space Station
   c. US Space Station

2. How many countries are building the ISS?
   a. more than five
   b. five
   c. less than five

3. When will the ISS be finished?
   a. in 2000
   b. in ten years
   c. in 2010

4. How fast does the ISS travel?
   a. 1,000,000 miles per hour
   b. 17,200 miles per hour
   c. 200 miles per hour

5. Where do the astronauts on the ISS sleep?
   a. on floating beds
   b. in floating sleeping bags
   c. in sleeping bags hooked to the wall

6. What do astronauts do with their clothes after they wear them?
   a. They throw them away.
   b. They wash them.
   c. They recycle them.

7. Why could "floating food" be dangerous on the ISS?
   a. It could go out into space.
   b. It could get into equipment.
   c. It could ruin the clothes.

8. How do the astronauts on the ISS eat soup?
   a. through straws
   b. with magnetic spoons
   c. in their sleeping bags

9. Do the astronauts wear the space suits inside the ISS?
   a. probably not
   b. yes
   c. only at dinner

10. What do the astronauts do when they have free time?
   a. fix and build the equipment
   b. eat and take showers
   c. send e-mails and watch DVDs

Pluto the Planet?

In 1930, Clyde Tombaugh discovered the ninth planet in Earth's solar system. He worked for the Lowell Observatory in Arizona. The people at the observatory wanted to name the planet. They asked for suggestions. They got ideas from all over the world. Venetia Burney, an eleven-year-old girl in England, thought of the name Pluto. A group of people chose three names from the suggestions. Every member of the Lowell Observatory got to vote for one of the names. The choices were Pluto, Minerva, and Cronus. Every person voted for Pluto.

From 1930 to 2006, students learned the nine planets in our solar system. They are: Mercury, Venus, Earth, Mars, Jupiter, Saturn, Uranus, Neptune, and Pluto. But…is Pluto really a planet?

Pluto is made of rocks and ice. It is very small compared to other objects in space. It is much smaller than Earth's moon. In the late 1990s, scientists started to discover many objects similar to Pluto in space. They questioned whether Pluto was a planet. A scientist discovered an object in 2005. Its name is Eris. It is larger than Pluto. This really made scientists wonder if Pluto really was a planet.

In 2006, the International Astronomical Union (IAU) created an official definition for the word "planet." The definition has three parts. 1) A planet is an object that orbits the sun. 2) It is large enough for its gravity to make it round. 3) It is not surrounded by a lot of other objects. Pluto does not fit the definition. It does orbit the sun, and it has its own gravity that makes it round. However, Pluto has many objects around it, unlike the other eight planets. For this reason, scientists in the IAU do not think Pluto is a planet.

The IAU created a new term for Pluto and other objects like it. IAU calls it a dwarf planet or a minor planet. Minor planets often have numbers. Scientists gave Pluto the number 134340.

Not everyone agrees with IAU's decisions. Many people still think Pluto is a planet. Scientists may be discussing Pluto for many years. What do you think?

Read each statement. Write *true* or *false*.

1. Venetia Burney discovered Pluto. _____

2. The Lowell Observatory is in Arizona. _____

3. Everyone at the Lowell Observatory voted for the name Pluto. _____

4. Neptune is not a planet. _____

5. The IAU doesn't think Pluto is a planet. _____

6. Pluto doesn't orbit the sun. _____

7. *Dwarf planet* and *minor planet* mean the same thing. _____

8. Earth is a dwarf planet. _____

9. Pluto's number is 1930. _____

10. No one thinks Pluto is a planet. _____

Twin Trips

Jenny and Jorge are identical twins. They built identical space shuttles in their backyard because they wanted to go into space. One day, their dog, Robo, got in one of the shuttles. He accidentally hit the control panel with his paw, and the space shuttle took off with a loud and brilliant blast. Jenny and Jorge watched the space shuttle fly through the air, but they couldn't stop it. They quickly got in the other shuttle and shot off into space to look for Robo.

Robo stopped at the International Space Station. The astronauts working there gave Robo a spacesuit and some space food for his trip. When Jenny and Jorge arrived at the space station, Robo had already left. The astronauts gave Jenny and Jorge space suits and some space food, too. They told them that Robo was heading for Mars.

Robo ate space food while he looked out the window. He flew by planets, moons, and asteroids. When he finally landed on Mars, he put on his space suit and played. He didn't see any Martian dogs, so he decided to leave. Jenny and Jorge landed on Mars. They saw Robo's paw prints on the red planet. They didn't see Robo, and they didn't see his space shuttle, so they got back into their shuttle.

Robo rocketed to Saturn. He liked the amazing rings around it. He couldn't land on Saturn because it is made of gas, so he decided to head to Neptune. Neptune was blue and beautiful, but it was extremely lonely on Neptune. He remembered that there was a famous dog named Pluto. He decided to go to Pluto to see if he could find Pluto the dog. Jenny and Jorge went to Neptune, too. They found a few pieces of space dog food that fell out of Robo's shuttle, but they didn't see Robo.

Robo took a space ball to Pluto in case he found Pluto the dog, but Pluto was also desolate. He couldn't play space ball by himself, so he left. He decided to go back to Earth because he was running out of space gas. Jenny and Jorge also went to Pluto. They found Robo's space ball, but they didn't find Robo. They put the space ball in their space shuttle and went home. When they got home, they found Robo in the front yard. They all played ball and decided they didn't want to go to outer space again.

Answer the questions below.

1. What did Robo hit with his paw?

_____

2. Where did Robo go first?

_____

3. What did the astronauts give Robo?

_____

4. What planet did Robo go to first?

_____

5. What did Jorge and Jenny see on Mars?

_____

6. Why couldn't Robo land on Saturn?

_____

7. What did Jorge and Jenny find on Neptune?

_____

8. What did Robo take to Pluto?

_____

9. What two phrases in paragraph four mean the same as *go to* and *went to*?

_____

10. What word in the last paragraph means that no one was on

Pluto?

_____

Comic Collections

Comic books started in the 1930s in the United States. Comic books can be funny, but usually they are serious stories. American comics often have superheroes. Spiderman and Superman are two popular superheroes who started in comic books. In 1938, Superman was one of the first superheroes to appear in comic books. Most comic books are for young adult readers, but there are also comic books that appeal to children and to adults.

Comic book historians divide comic books into different ages. The time before 1938 is the Platinum Age. The Golden Age is from the creation of Superman to the 1950s. This was the most popular age for buying comic books. The Silver Age is from the mid-1950s to the 1970s. The Bronze Age and the Modern Age follow the Silver Age. Marvel Comics was the most popular comic book company during the Golden Age and the Silver Age. It's still a popular company today. The characters created for Marvel include Superman, the Fantastic Four, X-Men, and the Incredible Hulk.

Comic book collecting is a very popular hobby. Comic book collectors gave the hobby a scientific-sounding name: panelology. In the 1960s, comic book fans and collectors began organizing comic book conferences. At the conferences, people discuss their favorite comic book characters and stories. Sometimes, comic book creators come to the conferences to talk to fans.

People collect comic books for different reasons. Many collectors collect them because they are interested in comic books. Others collect them because they feel nostalgia for the comics they read when they were young. Others collect them so that they can sell them later and make a profit. You can even buy comic book price guides to find out how much a comic book is worth! Today, many people buy and sell comic books online. If you do a quick search on the Internet, you'll find comic books for sale from $3 to $500.

Comic book collectors often want to preserve their comic books. They may put them in plastic bags or even buy special boxes for them. Sometimes, they mount them on acid-free boards to keep them flat.

Complete each sentence. Use the words in the word bank. The words in the word bank are similar to the words under the blanks.

ZAP! KERANG! SHAZAM!

| teenagers | protect | made | remember | costs |
| money | interest | separate | be | put |

1. Superman was one of the first superheroes to _____ in comic books.
   appear

2. Most comic books are for _____.
   young adults

3. There are also comic books that _____ children and adults.
   appeal to

4. Comic book historians _____ comic books into different ages.
   divide

5. The characters _____ for Marvel include Superman and the X-Men.
   created

6. Some people _____ the comics they read when they were young.
   feel nostalgia for

7. Others collect them so that they can sell them later and make _____.
   a profit

8. You can buy price guides to find out how much a comic book _____.
   is worth

9. Comic book collectors often want to _____ their comic books.
   preserve

10. Sometimes, they _____ them on acid-free boards to keep them flat.
    mount

From Finding to Fixing

David Michael has many unusual collections. He collects pinball machines, jukeboxes, and other unusual items. If you can put a coin in it, he probably collects it! He even has a machine that makes personalized stamps for a quarter.

David bought his first pinball machine in 1976, but his interest in them started before that. In 1957, his father gave him a pinball machine for his twelfth birthday. It only cost a nickel to play it. He immediately became interested in pinball machines. Later, he gave the machine to his cousin, but he decided he would buy another pinball machine when he bought his first house. He did just that. In 1976, he bought *Fireball*, one of the most collectible pinball machines. When he got it home, it didn't work, but he wasn't disappointed. He said, "When I opened up the front of the machine, I was fascinated by all of the wires!" He called the person who sold it to him. This person helped him fix it over the phone. David began a new hobby…fixing pinball machines.

"My interest in collecting pinball machines took off from there," he says. In 1980, he bought three broken machines. It took him a year to fix them because he taught himself how. He followed a schematic. A schematic is a map or diagram of the wiring system of a machine. Now he can fix machines faster. Sometimes he buys ten broken machines at a time!

He has bought, fixed, and sold over 350 pinball machines since 1980. He also began collecting, repairing, and selling jukeboxes. He buys and sells machines with advertisements in the newspaper, by going to trade shows, and sometimes on the Internet. He has met over 1,000 people through his hobby. He once drove over 800 miles from Michigan to Maryland to buy a 1960 motor scooter. Another time, he sent some machines by boat to a collector in Australia.

He says that his favorite part of collecting pinball machines is fixing them. He used to like to play them, but now he is more interested in buying old machines and getting them to work. His favorite item is *Fireball*, the first pinball machine that he bought. He still has it today. Even though he enjoys repairing machines and selling them to other people, he probably won't ever sell *Fireball*.

Read each question. Circle the correct answer.

1. What is the main idea of the reading?
  a. *Fireball*
  b. David and his collections
  c. Pinball trade shows

2. What does David collect?
  a. only pinball machines
  b. only jukeboxes
  c. pinball machines and jukeboxes

3. When did David receive his first pinball machine?
  a. in 1957
  b. in 1976
  c. in 1980

4. When did David buy *Fireball*?
  a. in 1957
  b. in 1960
  c. in 1976

5. What is a schematic?
  a. a map or diagram
  b. a pinball machine
  c. a video game

6. How many pinball machines has David had?
  a. about 1,000
  b. about 350
  c. about 800

7. What is a trade show?
  a. a conference where people buy and sell things
  b. a newspaper
  c. a website

8. What does David like best about collecting machines?
  a. playing them
  b. selling them
  c. fixing them

9. Why won't David sell *Fireball*?
  a. it's broken
  b. it's his favorite machine
  c. no one wants to buy it

10. Which word means the same as *repairing* in paragraph 5?
  a. selling
  b. buying
  c. fixing

A Closet Full of Collections

Deedee has several collections. She started collecting dogs when she was five. She has stuffed dogs, ceramic dogs, dog paintings, and dog toys. When her aunt gave her a mug with a dog on it for her sixth birthday, she decided to also collect mugs. She has three mugs with dogs on them. She has a mug with a cat on it. She has a mug with flowers on it. For her seventh birthday, her cousin gave her a personalized mug with her name on it.

Deedee then decided to collect things with her name on them. She has a sign on her bedroom door with her name on it. She has a monogrammed sweater. She has a beautiful necklace with her name. For her eighth birthday, her grandmother gave her a key chain with her name on it. Deedee thought it would be a good idea to collect key chains. She has key chains from different cities she's visited. She has plastic key chains, metal key chains, and leather key chains. She has red, blue, purple, green, and orange key chains. In fact, she has a key chain for every color of the rainbow. For her ninth birthday, her brother gave her a key chain with a stone on it.

What did Deedee do? She decided to collect stones. She has enormous stones and miniscule stones. She has found stones outside, and she has bought stones in stores. She has necklaces and rings with stones in them. For her tenth birthday, her grandfather gave her a lamp made of stones. Deedee had never seen a stone lamp before. She decided she wanted more lamps and started collecting those, too! She has tall lamps and short lamps. She has wide lamps and narrow lamps. She has a red, white, and blue lamp. She even has a lamp with a blue light bulb. For her eleventh birthday, her friend gave her a lamp adorned with a doll.

Of course, that was the start of Deedee's doll collection. She has dolls in fancy dresses and dolls in jeans. She has dolls with blonde, black, brown, and red hair. She even has a doll with purple hair. She has curly-haired dolls and straight-haired dolls.

Deedee's collections were getting out of control. She didn't have enough space for all of her collections. Her parents decided she needed to stop collecting. They had a plan. For her twelfth birthday, they bought her a doll with a dog. Deedee opened the gift. She loved it. She said, "I'm going to start collecting dogs!" She remembered she already had a dog collection. She spent the next year organizing her closets instead of collecting things.

Number the events in the correct order according to the story.

_____ Deedee turns eight.

_____ Deedee's friend gives her a lamp with a doll on it.

_____ Deedee gets a mug with her name on it.

_____ Deedee turns twelve.

_____ Deedee decides to collect key chains.

_____ Deedee's parents buy her a doll with a dog.

_____ Deedee starts to collect things with her name on them.

_____ Deedee starts to collect dogs.

_____ Deedee starts collecting stones.

_____ Deedee celebrates her sixth birthday.

_____ Deedee collects lamps.

_____ Deedee starts to collect mugs.

_____ Deedee's brother gives her a key chain with a stone on it.

_____ Deedee celebrates her tenth birthday.

Twin Cities?

There are many cities in the world that have the same name. For example, San José is the capital of the country Costa Rica. It is also the name of a city in California in the United States.

San José in Costa Rica has a population of about 310,000 people. It has a tropical climate, so it rains half of the year. Even in the rainy season, the days can be nice. Usually it rains very hard for a short period of time during the day, and then it gets sunny.

San Jose, California, is the tenth largest city in the United States, and the third largest city in California. It has a population of about 975,000 people. Its climate is similar to a desert because it doesn't get a lot of rain. On average, it's sunny 300 days a year.

Read the chart with information about other cities with the same name.

City	Location	Population	Climate	Interesting fact
St. Petersburg	Florida, US	about 250,000	warm to hot year-round	Many people in this city call it *St. Pete*.
	Russia	about 4,665,000	cold winters, cool summers	There have been many floods in this city.
Dublin	Ohio, US	about 35,000	four seasons with varying weather	John Shields, who was born in Dublin, Ireland, named it.
	Ireland	about 510,000	mild	It is the capital of Ireland.
Panama City	Florida, US	about 38,000	warm to hot year-round	It has many beaches nearby.
	Panama	about 800,000	tropical	This city is in Central America.
Paris	Texas, US	about 26,000	hot summers, mild winters	There are many tornados in this city.
	France	about 2,200,000	mild year-round	This city is the capital of France.
Berlin	Wisconsin, US	about 5,500	four seasons with varying weather	In the 1800s, farmers grew cranberries here. This helped the city grow.
	Germany	about 3,500,000	mild	It is the capital of Germany.

Answer the questions below.

1. Which city has the largest population?

_____

2. Which city has the smallest population?

_____

3. Which cities have over 1 million people?

_____

4. Which city has weather similar to Berlin, Wisconsin?

_____

5. Which cities have a lot of rain?

_____

6. Which city has a lot of tornados?

_____

7. Which city is the capital of France?

_____

8. Which city is in Central America?

_____

9. What city did John Shields name?

_____

10. Which city has a nickname? What is it?

_____

Castles Aren't Just for Kings and Queens

People often think of castles as magical places. When castles were first built, they had a practical purpose. Castles were actually homes of leaders, such as kings and queens. For this reason, castles were made so that they were hard to break into.

Castles are usually surrounded by high walls. Gates often cover the doors, so it's difficult to get into them without a key. They often have moats around them. Moats are ditches filled with water that surround a castle. There is a drawbridge that goes over the water and leads to the door. Years ago, kings and queens put the drawbridge down to enter the castle. Once inside, they drew the bridge up so that enemies couldn't get over the moat. Castles also have high towers. The towers were used as lookout spots. People who worked for a king or queen would look out of the windows in the towers so they could see if enemies were coming. The Citadel, a castle in Cairo, Egypt, has towers that are 80 feet high. Walls that are 30 feet high and 10 feet wide also surround it.

Today, some kings and queens still live in castles. For example, Queen Elizabeth and her family live in Buckingham Palace in London, England. They go to Windsor Castle in the country on the weekends, and the Queen even has a vacation castle in Scotland! It's called Balmoral Castle. Not only kings and queens live in castles. Some rich people buy castles that used to belong to royalty. Castles can be bought in countries such as France, Germany, England, and Italy.

Some castles have been turned into hotels. For instance, Ashford Castle, near Galway City, Ireland, is now a hotel. It has many rooms, two elegant restaurants, a tennis court, and a golf course. It's not cheap to stay there though! The least expensive room for one night is about $585 and the most expensive is about $1,540! Other castles have been turned into museums, such as the Turku Castle in Turku, Finland. Over 200,000 people visit this castle each year. It costs about $6 for a ticket to the museum.

You might not be able to buy a castle, and you might not have enough money to stay the night in one. However, you probably have enough money to visit a castle that is now a museum!

Label the picture. Use the words in the word bank.

wall   tower   moat   drawbridge   window   gate

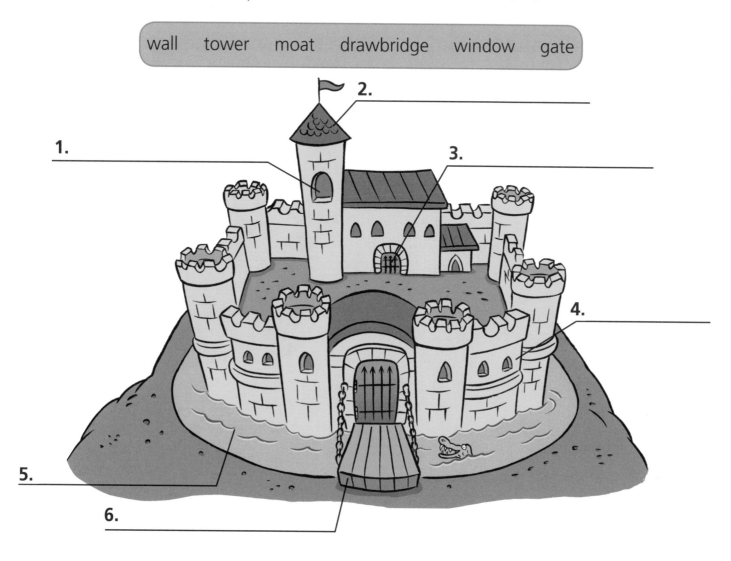

1.

2.

3.

4.

5.

6.

Read each statement. Write *true* or *false*.

7. Queen Elizabeth sometimes lives in Balmoral Castle. _____

8. Today, only kings and queens live in castles. _____

9. Turku Castle is a museum. _____

10. King Ashford lives in Ashford Castle. _____

Castles for a Kid

Tyler Forte lived in a small house with a big backyard. His older brother, Sam, had the bigger room, and Tyler's room was very small. To make him feel better, his parents painted the walls of his bedroom to make it look like a castle. He called it Castle Tye, and he loved playing in it.

When he was ten his mom had a baby girl named Lilly. She stayed in his parents' room for two years. Then one day, they told Sam and Tyler they would have to share a room because his sister needed her own room. Since Sam's room was bigger, Tyler had to give up his castle. He wasn't happy about this. Sam didn't like Tyler playing in their room. He was too old to play games that Tyler liked. He was usually listening to music or doing his homework. If Tyler was loud, he asked him to leave the room.

Tyler's parents decided he needed a place of his own. They built him a tree castle in a huge oak tree in the backyard. It had a ladder that hung down the tree, and it even had a tower. Tyler named this castle Castle Tye, too. He painted a big sign that said, "Keep Out," and hung it up on the outside of his tree castle. He picked up rocks from the yard, put them around the bottom of the tree, and pretended it was a moat. He used a board as a drawbridge to walk over the moat. Whenever he went up in his tree castle, he pulled the ladder up, so no one else could climb up.

Sam thought the tree castle was cool. He wanted to listen to his MP3 player or do his homework up there, but Tyler wouldn't let him. Lilly giggled when she saw the tree castle and said, "Up, please," but Tyler wouldn't let her in Castle Tye either.

After a month, Tyler got bored playing by himself in the tree castle. He decided that once in a while, it would be all right to have guests. Sometimes, his mom would bring Lilly up in the tree castle for lunch. His mom always cleaned up the mess Lilly made. Sam could come up, too, but only if he promised to play with Tyler. Sometimes, his dad would come up and fix up the tree castle. He let Tyler help him. Tyler decided a castle was better if you shared it. But once in a while, he still liked to go up there alone.

Complete each sentence. Use the phrases in the word bank.

> come up   bring up   go up   give up   fix up
> climb up   pull up   hang up   clean up   pick up

1. Tyler had to _____ his room for his sister.

2. He would _____ in his tree castle alone.

3. He would _____ the ladder to get to the top.

4. He would _____ the ladder once he got in the tree castle.

5. He decided to _____ a sign that said, "Keep Out."

6. He also decided to _____ rocks to make a moat.

7. Eventually, he decided that guests could
_____ once in a while.

8. Sometimes his mother would
_____ Lilly for lunch.

9. She would _____ the tree
castle before going back down.

10. Once in a while, his dad would
_____ the tree castle and let
Tyler help.

Baby Talk?

Sign language is a system of communication in which people use hand gestures to communicate. The first school for deaf children started in 1755 in Paris, France. The first deaf college started in the United States in 1864. There is not a universal sign language. Different countries have their own forms of sign language.

Not only deaf people learn sign language. People with deaf people in their families may learn sign language, and teachers who can hear may learn sign language to work with people who cannot hear. Today, many babies are learning sign language!

Many scientists feel that babies can communicate with sign language before they can speak. Sign language research for babies started with families with deaf children. Researchers realized that deaf babies were able to use signs earlier than when hearing babies could speak. Research into teaching signs to hearing babies began in the 1980s. Speaking is difficult because babies need to use their tongues, lips, and vocal cords. In sign language, they only need to use their hands. Some babies can use their hands to make signs when they are eight months old.

Today, many parents use signs with their babies. Some parents buy books or flash cards to teach babies basic signs. Others may take classes to learn signs to use with babies. They teach their babies common words to help them express what they need. Some common words are: *thirsty, tired, hungry, eat, more,* and *change my diaper.* They may also teach words of things that babies like. Some common words are: *puppy, kitty, TV, toy, mom,* and *dad.*

Parents are happy when their babies can communicate with them. Some parents begin using signs with babies when they are born. They are excited when their babies use signs before they are a year old. They like knowing exactly what their babies want or need even before they can talk!

Read each question. Circle the correct answer.

1. What is the main idea of the reading?
   a. the history of sign language
   b. babies learning sign language
   c. sign language around the world

2. What does *deaf* mean in paragraph 1?
   a. unable to hear
   b. young
   c. talkative

3. What does *universal* mean in paragraph 1?
   a. different countries
   b. one in the world
   c. France and the United States

4. When was the first school started for deaf children?
   a. in 1755
   b. in 1857
   c. in 1980

5. What do you need to use to speak sign language?
   a. your vocal cords
   b. your tongue
   c. your hands

6. When did research start for teaching hearing babies sign language?
   a. in the 1750s
   b. in the 1850s
   c. in the 1980s

7. How do parents learn sign language?
   a. from their babies
   b. from books or classes
   c. from their parents

8. What does *express* mean in paragraph 4?
   a. communicate
   b. teach
   c. learn

9. Babies can usually learn sign language before they can _____.
   a. crawl
   b. talk
   c. eat

10. Some parents start teaching their baby sign language when they are _____.
    a. eight months old
    b. a year old
    c. born

CAT

MOM

DAD

TIRED

Word!

English is an old language that began hundreds of years ago. New words are always being added to the English language. They come from many different places.

Other Languages

Sometimes words from other languages are used a lot in English. These words become English words. The word *ballet* is French, and the word *hamburger* is German. These words have been used in English for a long time, but there are newer words in English from other languages. For example, the word *barrio* is in English dictionaries. It is a Spanish word that means neighborhood. *Feng shui* is a Chinese phrase. It means something is arranged in a pleasant way. This word is also in modern English dictionaries.

Technology

There are many new words in English because of computers. For example, fifty years ago the word *mouse* was only used for a small rodent. Now it is also used for a device that controls the movements on a computer. Other "old" words have new meanings because of technology—for example: *Blackberry, chat, monitor, memory,* and *chip*. There are other words that are new to English because of computers. For example: *download, Internet, e-mail,* and *CD-ROM*.

Brand Names

Sometimes a brand name of an item is so popular that many people use the name for the item. For example, Kleenex® is a company that makes tissues. Many people call all tissues Kleenex® even though it is not the real word for tissue. Other examples of these kinds of words are: *Walkman®* (audio player), *Rollerblade®* (in-line skates), *Xerox®* (photocopy), and *Google®* (search the Internet).

Slang

Slang means that a word is not Standard English. Teenagers often use slang. Sometimes a slang word is used so much over time that it is added to the dictionary. Some slang words stay popular for a long time and others for a short time. For example, *cool* and *rad* were slang words used for *excellent*. Teenagers started saying *cool* in the 1950s, and people of many ages still say *cool* today. *Rad* was started in the 1980s, but not many people used the word after 1990. Other popular slang words are: *chill* (calm down), *crash* (go to sleep), and *dude* (a person).

English is a language that keeps growing. Do you know any "new" English words?

Complete each sentence. Use the words or phrases in the word bank. Then check whether the word came from another language, technology, or slang.

Blackberry   dude   e-mailed   hamburger   monitor
cool   barrio   chill   download   feng shui

	Another Language	Technology	Slang
1. Did you _____ the photo that Todd e-mailed you?			
2. Tom had a _____ and French fries for lunch.			
3. Does Rita live in your _____?			
4. You seem angry. Please _____.			
5. Kate sent me a message on my _____.			
6. Lee bought a big _____ for her computer. Now she can see her photos better.			
7. Your new backpack is so _____.			
8. Who is that _____ in the green coat?			
9. My mom wants to redecorate our house. She bought a book about _____.			
10. Marisa _____ me yesterday, but I didn't write back yet.			

Coded Communication

Oliver and Olivia are neighbors, and they are also good friends. They talk to each other every day. They walk to school together and have long conversations. At night, they talk to each other on the phone or send each other text messages. One day, Olivia's parents decided she should try not to talk on the phone so much. Oliver and Olivia took two cans and tied them to a long string. They talked to each other using the cans through their bedroom windows. One day, the string broke. They decided to make up signs and talk to each other using their hands. They spoke this way at night for several weeks. In the winter, it got dark earlier at night and they couldn't see each other's hands anymore. They decided to e-mail each other.

Last summer, Oliver spent the summer away at camp. He couldn't take his cell phone, and the camp didn't have computers. Oliver and Olivia wrote each other postcards all summer. He wrote about all the fun things he was doing at summer camp, and she wrote him about what was going on in the neighborhood.

When Oliver got home, he came up with an idea. He decided they should create a secret code to communicate. They made up a code together. They decided to write backwards. They left each other messages every day. Oliver's brother figured out the code, so Olivia made up a new code. They gave each letter of the alphabet a number. They wrote to each other using numbers instead of letters. Olivia's older sister figured out the code. They didn't know what to do. They didn't want anyone else to know their code.

They decided it would be fun to make up their own language. They called it Olive. They wrote each other messages in Olive. They e-mailed each other in Olive. They even spoke Olive together at school and at home. Their parents and friends got frustrated because they couldn't understand what they were saying. Olivia and Oliver thought it was humorous. They started speaking Olive at school. The teacher didn't understand what they were saying. They decided to answer the questions on an English test in Olive. They both failed the test because the teacher didn't understand the answers. They decided it was better to speak and write in English.

Answer the questions below.

1. Who was not allowed to talk on the phone?

_____

2. Why did Oliver and Olivia stop using the cans?

_____

3. Why did they stop using sign language?

_____

4. Who went to summer camp?

_____

5. How did Oliver and Olivia communicate in the summer?

_____

6. Who decided they should write in code?

_____

7. Who figured out the backwards code?

_____

8. What word in paragraph 4 means the same as *upset*?

_____

9. What word in paragraph 4 means the same as *funny*?

_____

10. Who couldn't understand Olive?

_____

How to Bowl

• Find a couple of friends and go to your nearest bowling alley. If you don't have a bowling ball, you can rent one. You can also rent bowling shoes. You can't wear the shoes you wear on the street in a bowling alley.

• Each group of bowlers has its own lane, and you and your friends will take turns bowling in one lane. Decide who will go first, second, third, and so on, and write the names on the scorecard.

• The first person goes to the lane and rolls the bowling ball down the lane. There are ten pins at the end of the lane that he or she tries to knock down. The person gets two turns to try to knock down the pins. Then it's the next person's turn to try.

• A scorekeeper writes down how many pins the player knocks down in the first roll. Then he or she adds the number of pins knocked down in the second roll. This is the total number of points for the player. If a player doesn't knock down any pins, it's called a *gutter ball*. A gutter ball is worth zero points. If a player knocks down all ten pins in two rolls, it is called a *spare*. A slash (/) is used to show a spare on the scorecard. It's good to get a spare because you get a bonus. If a player knocks  down all ten pins in one roll, it's called a *strike*. An X is used to show a strike on the scorecard. A strike is worth a bigger bonus!

• After every player has two rolls, the first person goes again. Each turn (two rolls) is called a *frame*. There are ten frames in bowling. That means each person gets ten turns. If a person gets a spare in the tenth frame, he or she gets to roll the ball one more time to try and get extra points. If a person gets a strike in the tenth frame, he or she gets to roll the ball two more times to try and get more points. The person with the highest score at the end of the game wins. The highest possible score in bowling is 300 points. To get 300 points, you have to roll strikes for every single frame!

• When you leave, don't forget to return the bowling shoes you rented!

Label the picture. Use the words in the word bank.

| bowling ball | strike | bowler | pins | gutter |
| lane | score card | spare | bowling shoes | |

1. _____

2. _____

3. _____

4. _____

5. _____

6. _____

7. _____

Read each statement. Write *true* or *false*.

8. A strike is knocking down ten pins in one roll.   _____

9. A spare is worth a bigger bonus than a strike.   _____

10. A gutter ball is worth less than a spare.   _____

The Butterfly and the Bee

Have you ever heard of Cassius Clay? How about Muhammad Ali? It's the same person! Cassius was born on January 17, 1942, and he changed his name to Muhammad in 1964.

Muhammad Ali is a famous boxer. He is one of the most famous and popular boxers in the world. His boxing career started because of a stolen bike! When Cassius was twelve years old, a police officer saw him after someone had stolen his bike. Cassius was very upset. The officer felt sorry for him. He took him to a boxing trainer, Fred Stoner, who was one of his friends. Fred trained Cassius during his amateur boxing career. He won 100 boxing matches, and only lost five. He even won an Olympic gold medal in 1960.

In his professional career, Ali won the World Heavyweight Championship three times. He was a great boxer. He was known for his style in and out of the boxing ring. He was famous for many sayings about his boxing such as: "I'm so fast that last night I turned off the light switch in my hotel room and was in bed before the room was dark," and "I'll be floating like a butterfly and stinging like a bee." He also had important things to say about life, such as: "I wish people would love everybody else the way they love me. It would be a better world," and "A man who views the world the same at fifty as he did at twenty has wasted thirty years of his life."

Ali retired from boxing in 1981. He ended his professional career with 56 wins and five losses. He now has Parkinson's syndrome, a disease that affects movement. He still makes many public appearances and supports civil rights. His daughter, Laila Ali, became a boxer in 1999.

Ali had a long career and continues to be a boxing legend, and it all started with a stolen bike!

Match each word to its defintion. Write the letter on the line.

1. _____ upset

2. _____ train

3. _____ amateur

4. _____ match

5. _____ professional

6. _____ sayings

7. _____ views

8. _____ retired

9. _____ legend

10. _____ support

a. not professional, not getting paid for doing something

b. words someone says that may become famous

c. instruct

d. well-known or famous person

e. sees

f. sad and angry

g. game or competition

h. defend or argue for

i. doing something as a career for money

j. stopped working

Not Fair!

Jennifer and Brett go to Valley Middle School, and their school has a lot of sports teams. It has some sports for both boys and girls, such as soccer, tennis, and basketball. It has some sports only for boys, like baseball and football. It has some sports only for girls, such as volleyball and gymnastics.

Jennifer plays football at the park with her brothers every weekend. One day she says, "Joe, I want to be on the school football team."

Her brother says, "Girls can't play football on real teams. It's for boys."

"That's not fair," says Jennifer, and she angrily stomps away.

Brett's family has a volleyball net in the backyard, and he plays volleyball a lot with his cousins. One day he says, "Tanya, I want to play volleyball on the school team."

His cousin says, "You can't play volleyball on your school's team. It only has a team for girls."

"That's not fair," says Brett, and he furiously stomps away.

Brett runs into Jennifer walking to school the next day. He asks, "Why do you look so sad?"

She answers, "Because I want to play football on the school's team, and it's only for boys."

"Really? You know, I want to play volleyball, but it's only for girls. I have an idea. Meet me after school."

Jennifer meets Brett after school. He thinks he should pretend he's Jennifer and Jennifer should pretend she's him, so they can try out for the teams they want to be on. But Jennifer doesn't look like a boy at all, and Brett looks nothing like a girl.

They decide to show up and try out for the teams as themselves. All the boys look at Jennifer strangely at football try outs, but they are surprised. She can tackle, and she can throw the ball far. The coach says she can be on the team. Brett has as a similar experience trying out for the volleyball team. The coach is impressed with how well he can spike the ball. She says he can be on the team.

Jennifer isn't the best football player on the team, but she's very good. She scored a touchdown in the first football game. Brett isn't the best volleyball player on the team, but he is very good. He scored three points in the first game by spiking the ball.

They hope next year more girls will try out for football and more boys will try out for volleyball.

Read each question. Circle the correct answer.

1. Who can play on the soccer team at Valley Middle School?
   a. only boys
   b. only girls
   c. girls and boys

2. Who is Joe?
   a. Jennifer's brother
   b. Jennifer's cousin
   c. Brett's brother

3. Who does Brett play volleyball with?
   a. only Tanya
   b. his brothers
   c. Tanya and other cousins

4. Which word means the same as *angrily* in paragraph 4?
   a. angry
   b. furiously
   c. stomps

5. What does *pretend* mean in paragraph 11?
   a. to act like someone else
   b. to play on the opposite team
   c. to act like a professional player

6. What do Brett and Jennifer decide to do?
   a. try out for the teams they want to be on
   b. pretend to be the other person
   c. tackle the coaches

7. What has about the same meaning as *show up* in paragraph 12?
   a. try out
   b. come
   c. leave

8. What did Jennifer do at the first football game?
   a. watch her brother play
   b. spike the ball
   c. make a touchdown

9. What did Brett do at the first volleyball game?
   a. make three points
   b. make a touchdown
   c. try out for the team

10. Who is the best football player on the team?
   a. Jennifer
   b. Brett
   c. unknown

A Very Busy Volunteer

Helen Monson has always been interested in helping her community. Her first volunteer experience was for the American Red Cross when she was in high school. When she was an elementary school teacher, she also found time to volunteer. One year, she organized a Super Saturday fun day for kids in the community. She also used to volunteer at the annual Mint Festival. One summer she served food, another year she organized an art program, and she even scooped up ice cream one year!

After she retired, she started volunteering at a nursing facility. When her father was older, he was not able to see as well as he used to, which made her sad because he had always enjoyed reading. She decided it would be fun to read to elderly people in her community. She also helped one woman write her biography. Ann was almost 100 years old, and Helen wrote down information about her life when she visited her. She put the information in a book. Ann was very excited to share her life story with her children and grandchildren.

After Hurricane Katrina devastated cities in the southern part of the United States, Helen volunteered again with the American Red Cross. She worked on a food drive, answered phones, and wrote receipts for donations. She says, "I have always liked the Red Cross because the organization helps people in need no matter what."

One day Helen read an article in the newspaper about refugees needing to learn English. Now, she meets once a week with Sahra, a 38-year-old woman from Somalia. Sahra is living and working in a town about 30 minutes from where Helen lives. They work on reading and writing skills. Helen gave Sahra a disposable camera and asked her to take pictures of her daily life. She developed the pictures, and then asked Sahra questions about them. Finally, they wrote a book together and used the photos to illustrate the words. This helped Sahra learn useful words about her everyday life.

Helen says, "The most rewarding part of volunteer work is becoming friends with the people I help. They enrich my life as much as I enrich theirs." When asked what advice she has for people who want to volunteer she says, "Just do it!"

Read each statement. Check whether it is a *fact* or an *inference*.

	Fact	Inference
1. Helen enjoyed teaching children.		
2. The Mint Festival happens once a year.		
3. Helen helped Ann write a book about her life.		
4. Ann's grandchildren read the book.		
5. People donated money to the Red Cross after Hurricane Katrina.		
6. Helen answered questions about Hurricane Katrina on the phone at the Red Cross.		
7. Sahra appreciates Helen's help.		
8. The book helped Sahra learn English.		
9. Helen thinks volunteer work is rewarding.		
10. Helen will continue doing other kinds of volunteer work in the future.		

Helping Hands

There are many ways you can help in your community or in the world. Here are some ideas.

Adopt Something

• You can adopt a pet. Go to an animal shelter and adopt a homeless cat or dog. You will save an animal. You can give it a good home and a lot of love.

• You can adopt other animals, too. You can even adopt a whale! No, you don't bring the whale to your house! You donate money to an organization that helps whales. The organization will combine your donation with other people's money and help a whale in danger. They will even send you a picture of the whale.

• You can adopt a tree! Some organizations have websites where you can choose a tree you want to adopt by clicking on its picture. You send money to the organization, and it goes to protecting your tree.

• You can adopt a highway with other people! In this program, you and others keep a section of a highway or road looking nice. You pick up trash on the side of your part of the road. You may also plant trees and flowers to make it look nicer.

Volunteer Your Time

• You don't have to donate money to help in your community. There are many ways you can volunteer your time. You can go to a nursing facility in your community. Many older people who live in nursing facilities are lonely. You can volunteer to visit an older person once a week. You can talk with the person. You may even read to people who cannot see very well or write letters for people.

• Volunteer to help keep your park clean. You can pick up litter in your park or clean graffiti. Check with your local park to see if it has a volunteer organization.

Give Something Away

• You can donate your clothes to organizations. They give clothes to people who need them. Make sure the clothes are clean and not torn.

• You can give away toys you don't use anymore. Make sure they're clean and not broken. Many organizations collect toys around the holidays or during other times of the year.

• Some places, like libraries, collect books. You could give books you've read to someone else to read and enjoy!

Complete the chart with ways you can help your community according to the reading.

Ways to Help

ADOPT	
CLEAN	
VOLUNTEER	
DONATE	
PLANT	

Paula's Pets

Paula Pines is very kind and loves pets. For her fifth birthday, she got a cat. It was fluffy and frisky, and she named it Perry. She lived with Perry in peace until she was ten. Then she and Perry found another cat. They were walking in the park, and heard a little "meow." They saw a cute, cuddly kitten. It was a stray, and it didn't have a home. Paula took it home, and her parents said she could keep it. They took it to a veterinarian to make sure it was healthy. Paula named the kitten Prince.

Paula, Perry, and Prince lived in peace for a few months. Then one day, on her way home from school, Paula heard a "meow" coming from a bush. She found a furry and friendly cat. She took it home and went with her parents to the veterinarian. The vet gave the cat a few shots, and Paula took the cat home. She named it Penelope.

Paula, Perry, Prince, and Penelope lived in peace for a few weeks. Then one day, on her way home from soccer practice, she heard a "meow" coming from up in a tree. She climbed the tree and brought down a small and silky kitten. She took it home, and her frustrated parents said, "Enough!" They understood that she wanted to help the animals, but they couldn't afford how expensive it was to feed them all and take them to the vet. Paula had an idea.

She started an "Adopt-A-Kitten" program. She charged people only the price of the veterinarian visit, so she could make sure the cats were healthy before she gave them away. Her parents thought it was a great idea and that she was very creative. They helped her make signs, and she advertised in the neighborhood. Her older sister interviewed people to make sure they would give the cats good homes.

Paula gave the small and silky kitten to a boy who lived on her block. She decided to let him give the pet a name, even though she secretly called the kitten Penny. She rescued many more cats and kittens and found homes for them all. Her parents let her keep Perry, Prince, and Penelope, and they lived in peace.

Complete the chart with character descriptions from the story.
Use the words in the word bank.

frustrated	kind	furry	silky	frisky	cute
small	fluffy	creative	cuddly	friendly	understanding

Paula	_____, _____
Perry	_____, _____
Prince	_____, _____
Penelope	_____, _____
Paula's parents	_____, _____
"Penny"	_____, _____

Treasure Time!

A treasure is something of great worth or value which is often lost for a period of time and discovered years later. There are many stories, both factual and fictitious, of people looking for missing treasures. *Treasure Island* is a famous book from 1883 about a boy who searches for a treasure. Treasure stories often take place in the ocean with pirates or on deserted islands. Many times in these stories a person looks for a treasure using a map. The map has clues as to where the treasure is hidden. These maps are called treasure maps. Many times the treasure is buried in the ground, so it is called a buried treasure.

Indiana Jones movies about treasure hunting were popular in the 1980s. The *Pirates of the Caribbean* movies started in 2003 and are popular treasure-hunting movies involving pirates. They are fantasy movies, and even though the *Indiana Jones* movies are fiction, the main character had a real-life job. Indiana Jones was an archeologist. Many archeologists are called treasure hunters because it's their job to find treasures from the past. However, these treasures aren't just jewels and don't make them rich.

Archeologists find items from the past to answer questions about how people lived. They may find clothing, pots, and even jewelry or gold. Archeologists don't keep the treasures they find. They study them and eventually give them to museums for people to see.

You don't have to be a pirate or an archeologist to look for treasures. Some people buy metal detectors and look for treasures on the beach! They hope to find old, valuable coins or lost rings to make them wealthy. Others look for treasures in antique stores. They might buy an old lamp or painting, hoping it's worth a lot of money. Some people buy items now that may be treasures in the future. For example, you may buy a painting by an artist who isn't famous. If the artist becomes famous, your painting may become a treasure!

Treasures are everywhere...in books, in movies, in museums, and maybe even at the beach!

Match each word to its synonym. Write the letter on the line. Use the context in the reading to help you.

1. _____ worth

2. _____ lost

3. _____ discover

4. _____ search

5. _____ fantasy

6. _____ factual

7. _____ treasure

8. _____ deserted

9. _____ antique

10. _____ archeologist

a. fictitious

b. old

c. look for

d. value

e. riches

f. find

g. treasure hunter

h. missing

i. abandoned

j. real-life

Solid Gold

Gold is a very valuable metal. It is used for jewelry, but it also has been used as a form of money. At one time, people traded gold for other items, such as food or clothing. Gold coins became popular as a form of money. Gold was a good metal for coins because it is not affected by the air or even pollution. It lasts for a very long time, but it is very soft. Gold was mixed with other metals to make the coins harder. Gold is very heavy, so today coins are made out of lighter and cheaper metals. Paper, like the dollar bill, is also used for money.

Even though gold coins are not exchanged, many countries keep bars of gold in banks. The coins and paper we use for money represent gold that really exists. Gold is stored in vaults or safes in national banks. These are gold reserves. The United States has the largest amount of gold in reserves in the world. The largest amount of gold is stored in New York City, New York. The second largest amount is stored in Fort Knox, Kentucky. Germany, France, Italy, Switzerland, Japan, the Netherlands, and China are all in the top ten for amounts of gold they have in reserves.

The gold is stored in bars that look like bricks. Each brick usually weighs about 27.5 pounds. A gold brick is about seven inches long, $3\frac{5}{8}$ inches wide, and $1\frac{3}{4}$ inches tall. They look similar to the bricks used to build a house, but they are solid gold. Each brick is worth about $241,000.

Security is serious at gold reserves. For example, in the vault in Fort Knox, the gold is stored below the ground. The vault cannot be blasted through, and the door to the vault weighs 24.6 tons. That's more than the weight of three elephants! There are fences around the building and security guards and video cameras everywhere. There is not one person that knows the combination to the vault. Several different people have parts of the combination, and they must all enter their part for anyone to enter the vault. No visitors are allowed.

Gold is still very valuable and popular even though it is not used in coins. People can even buy small gold bars. Sometimes they store them in safes in banks.

Read each question. Circle the correct answer.

1. What is the main idea of the reading?
   a. gold jewelry
   b. uses of gold
   c. where and how gold is stored

2. What are coins made out of today?
   a. gold
   b. cheap metals
   c. paper

3. Which of the following sentences is **not** true about gold?
   a. It's valuable.
   b. It's hard.
   c. It's a metal.

4. What word in paragraph 2 means the same as *vault*?
   a. safe
   b. bank
   c. reserve

5. What is a reserve?
   a. a gold coin
   b. a place where gold is stored
   c. the largest amount of gold

6. Which country has the largest amount of gold in reserves in the world?
   a. Japan
   b. New York
   c. the Unites States

7. How much does a gold brick usually weigh?
   a. about as much as a brick for a house
   b. about 7 inches
   c. about 27.5 pounds

8. How much does the door to the vault at Fort Knox weigh?
   a. about as much as one elephant
   b. 26.4 tons
   c. 241,000 pounds

9. What does *combination* mean in paragraph 4?
   a. a code to open something
   b. doing something together
   c. a heavy door

10. Which of the following are **not** at the Fort Knox gold reserve?
   a. gold bars and fences
   b. elephants and visitors
   c. security guards and video cameras

Fable of Fabian and Friendship

Fabian Phillips was famous four hundred years ago. He wasn't born famous, but he became famous when he found gold dust. His parents were the King and Queen of Fluorescentville, a small sunny village near a dark forest. Fabian had a sister named Farah and a brother named Franklin. One day, their parents sent them out to see who could find the best treasure.

Franklin, Farah, and Fabian went deep into the forest. Franklin saw a fairy sitting on a branch of a gigantic tree. He said, "Hello, fairy. Can you help me? I'm looking for a treasure to take to my parents."

The fairy said, "There is a treasure chest filled with gold in a cave by the river. Your parents will be happy with the gift of gold coins." The fairy took Franklin to the cave.

Next, Farah saw an elf sitting on top of a large rock. She said, "Hello, elf. Can you help me? I'm looking for a treasure to take to my parents."

The elf said, "There is a treasure chest buried in the ground not far from here. It's filled with gold jewelry. Your parents will be happy with the gift of gold jewelry." The elf took Farah to the buried treasure.

Finally, Fabian found two goblins sitting on a large box near a bush. He said, "Hello, goblins. Can you help me? I'm looking for a treasure to take to my parents."

The goblins said, "Tell your parents that the best treasure in the world is friendship. Take this box of gold dust. It's not valuable, but you'll figure out what to do with it."

Back home, Franklin presented the gold coins to his parents and told them they would be the richest people in the world. Farah gave her parents the gold jewelry and told them they would be the most beautiful people in the world. Fabian told his parents that friendship was the best treasure in the world. He said, "We are rich because we have a lot of wonderful friends."

The King and Queen agreed with Fabian. They decided to have a party to celebrate friendship, and they invited all of their friends. Everyone had a splendid time. Fabian took out the box of gold dust and threw it in the air. Everyone laughed and danced. They looked beautiful covered in gold dust. To this day, people in Flourescentville celebrate friendship once a year because of Fabian.

Number the events in the correct order according to the story.

_____ Farah gave her parents gold jewelry.

_____ Fabian saw two goblins.

_____ Franklin found a fairy.

_____ Fabian threw gold dust at the party.

_____ The children went into the forest.

_____ The fairy led Franklin to a cave with a treasure chest in it.

_____ The King and Queen had a party.

_____ An elf took Farah to treasure buried in the ground.

_____ Fabian told his parents that friendship is the best treasure in the world.

_____ Franklin gave his parents gold coins.

_____ The King and Queen asked their children to find treasures.

_____ The goblins told Fabian that friendship is the best treasure in the world.

Marine Life

The oceans of the world cover 71 percent of the globe. They provide a way to get from one continent to the other on ships. They are also used for entertainment. People swim, ski, and kayak in the ocean. They also provide food. Many people eat fish and other things that live in the ocean, such as seaweed. The ocean also provides jobs. You may instantly think of fishermen or coastguards, but have you heard of marine biologists?

Marine biologists study the plants and animals that live in the ocean. Some study large ocean creatures such as whales and giant squids. Others study things that are too small to see without a microscope.

Marine biologists study all kinds of animals that live in the ocean. There are mammals, fish, seabirds, and even reptiles that live under water! You have probably heard of many of the mammals that live in the ocean, like whales, dolphins, seals, and manatees. You probably know the names of many fish, too. Tuna, sharks, barracuda, and cod are fish that marine biologists study. They also study unusual fish, such as anemonefish. These are also called clownfish because of their bright colors. Seabirds include penguins and auks. Marine biologists have figured out that even though auks look like penguins, they are very different. Penguins can't fly, but auks can swim under water and fly in the air. Reptiles that live in the ocean include sea snakes, sea turtles, and saltwater crocodiles. As you can imagine, a marine biologist's job can be dangerous!

Marine biologists are important because their work helps in many ways. They may help keep food found in the ocean safe for humans to eat. They may also help endangered species in the ocean. Sometimes they even discover medicines found in the ocean that may help people.

Jacques Cousteau was a famous marine biologist from France. He lived from 1910 to 1997. He not only studied the ocean and tried to protect it, he also told many people about ocean life. He made many movies about the ocean that were on TV. In 1973, he and his two sons created the Cousteau Society. It's an organization that fights to protect ocean life.

The oceans of the world are enormous, but we can learn a lot about them from marine biologists.

Match each topic to two supporting details. Write the letter on the line.

Topics:

1. _____ _____   Jobs involving the ocean

2. _____ _____   What marine biologists do

3. _____ _____   Ocean animals

4. _____ _____   How marine biologists help

5. _____ _____   Jacques Cousteau's life

Supporting details:
a. They study microscopic things.

b. Auks can swim and fly.

c. An unusual job is a marine biologist.

d. They study large animals.

e. He made movies about the ocean.

f. Fishermen and coastguards are common jobs.

g. They help endangered species.

h. He started an organization to protect ocean life.

i. Clownfish are unusual fish.

k. They discover medicine.

See the Seahorses?

Seahorses aren't horses that live in the ocean or the sea. They are fish. In fact, they are very small fish. They are usually between $\frac{1}{2}$ inch and $1\frac{1}{2}$ inches long. They are called seahorses because their faces look like that of a horse. They actually have gills and fins like other fish do. Some seahorses are very hard to see because they are transparent.

Seahorses don't have teeth, so they suck food through their long snouts. They eat very small ocean creatures but, in turn, are eaten by larger creatures. Seahorses move very slowly, so they have many enemies. Eels, clownfish, tuna, octopi, squid, sea turtles, and penguins all eat seahorses. Even though seahorses are slow, they have a way of protecting themselves. They can move their eyes quickly in many directions without moving their body. One eye can move in one direction while the other eye moves in the opposite direction. They can see their enemies coming from many directions and remain still so that the enemies don't notice them.

Seahorses are unusual because they look like many different animals. You already know their heads look like a horse's head. Their eyes move and look like a chameleon's eyes. Their tails look like a monkey's tail, and they have pouches like a kangaroo's!

Seahorses are also unique because male seahorses have the babies. Babies are immediately independent when they are born. They don't need their parents and live on their own in the ocean.

Wild seahorses do not make good pets. They do not live very long in aquariums. Life outside of the ocean causes stress and makes seahorses get diseases easily. However, many seahorses have been domesticated. This means that they are born in aquariums, not in the ocean. It's similar to the difference between a dog that is a pet and a wolf in the wild. They are in the same family, but they are very different. Domesticated seahorses make good pets if they are given proper care.

Marine biologists are still learning a lot about seahorses. So far, they know there are  34 different kinds of seahorses, but they think there are many more. Scientists are not even sure how long seahorses live. They think they live between one and five years. It's difficult to know for sure because seahorses are most often studied in captivity, but they live longer in the wild.

Complete the chart with information from the reading.

Seahorse Facts

1. Length	
2. What they eat	
3. Lifespan	
4. Number of known kinds	

Match each word to its definiton. Write the letter on the line.

5. _____ transparent   **a.** something harmful

6. _____ snout   **b.** not in the wild

7. _____ enemy   **c.** stay

8. _____ remain   **d.** see-through

9. _____ unique   **e.** unusual

10. _____ captivity   **f.** nose

Sea Dreams

1 I see the sea and it comes to me
2 Visions of life, waves of glee
3 Blue and green, green and gray
4 Whales leaping, dolphins at play

5 Sea breezes on a sandy shore
6 Seashells, pebbles, sand castles galore!
7 Sunscreen and blankets, even a pail
8 Deep-sea dives and boats that sail

9 Sea snakes and eels swim on by
10 I see clownfish and tuna in my eye
11 Seahorses stay still, but small fish flee
12 I see octopus, squid, and a manatee

13 Off in the distance, I see a ship
14 Marine biologists on a long sea trip
15 On board is Jacques Cousteau
16 He sails on by and waves hello

17 Blue and green, green and gray
18 Animals and people, all at play
19 I see the sea and it comes to me
20 Visions of life, waves of glee

Read each question. Circle the correct answer.

1. What does the title tell you about the poem?
 a. the author is imagining the sea
 b. the author is dreaming about sharks
 c. the author is a marine biologist

2. What does *glee* mean in line 2?
 a. whales
 b. pictures
 c. happiness

3. What does *galore* mean in line 6?
 a. a lot of
 b. wind
 c. sunny

4. What does *in my eye* mean in line 10?
 a. the author has sand in her eye
 b. the author is imagining clownfish and tuna
 c. the clownfish and tuna have eyes

5. What does *flee* mean in line 11?
 a. go away
 b. remain still
 c. stay in one place

6. What does *on board* mean in line 15?
 a. in the sea
 b. on the ship
 c. for a long time

7. Cousteau is a French name that you might not know how to pronounce. Based on the structure of the poem, what word does it rhyme with?
 a. Jacques
 b. hello
 c. trip

8. What does the author think of when she thinks of the sea?
 a. things people do
 b. animals and nature
 c. both a and b

9. What is the mood of the poem?
 a. playful and happy
 b. sad and concerned
 c. angry and colorful

10. What is probably the author's purpose for writing the poem?
 a. to encourage people to study marine biology
 b. to share information about her hero, Jacques Cousteau
 c. to share her memories and visions of the sea

The Invention of Ice Cream

You've probably had ice cream before, and you might even know what it's made from. Maybe you've even made it yourself at home! But have you ever wondered where it came from? Did your great-grandparents eat ice cream? Did people eat it 500 years ago? Did George Washington, the first president of the United States, eat ice cream?

Ice cream is made from milk, sugar, and other ingredients to give it flavor. For example, vanilla beans are added to the mixture for vanilla ice cream, and fresh strawberries might be used to make strawberry ice cream. The mixture is stirred slowly in a very cool place so that it doesn't turn to ice while it's getting cold.

But when was ice cream invented? Ice cream might have existed as many as 4,000 years ago. In ancient Greece, people bought ice mixed with honey and fruit in the markets. The first ice cream was more like flavored ice or snow cones than the ice cream people eat today. In Ecuador, ice cream was made by adding fruit juice to snow taken from the top of a volcano. In China, people put snow, fruit juice, and syrup in a container and poured a chemical over the outside of the container. The chemical made the temperature of the mixture drop below freezing. They stirred the mixture while the chemical was making it freeze. Later, they added milk to the mixture. This is similar to what ice cream is like today.

Ice cream machines were invented in the 1840s. This made ice cream more popular, and many ice cream shops opened. Some of the first ice cream shops in the United States were in New York City. In the 1900s, people started having ice cream at home because they could keep it in their freezers.

Soft ice cream was invented in England. Some people found a way to double the amount of air in the mixture to make the ice cream softer and lighter. Soft ice cream usually comes out of a machine because it is too soft to scoop like hard ice cream.

So your great-grandparents probably did eat ice cream. George Washington definitely ate it. In fact, it was one of his favorite foods!

Read each statement. Write *true*, *false*, or *no information*.

1. Strawberry ice cream was popular in Greece. _____

2. Vanilla beans can be used to make vanilla ice cream. _____

3. Years ago, ice cream was mixed inside a volcano. _____

4. People in China used a chemical to make ice cream freeze. _____

5. Ice cream machines were invented in the 1900s. _____

6. The invention of the ice cream machine made ice cream more popular.
_____

7. There were 1,000 ice cream shops in New York City in the 1900s.
_____

8. Soft ice cream was invented in China. _____

9. Soft ice cream has twice as much air as hard ice cream. _____

10. George Washington's great-grandfather loved ice cream. _____

We All Scream for Ice Cream!

Ice cream comes in many forms. There's hard ice cream and soft ice cream. There are ice cream cones, ice cream sandwiches, ice cream sundaes, and ice cream bars. It seems every few years, someone invents a new way to serve and eat ice cream!

In the 1950s, ice cream sodas were popular. An ice cream soda is just what it sounds like—a couple of scoops of your favorite ice cream in your favorite soda! People started dipping soft ice cream cones in chocolate syrups or nuts. For years, it was common to have real chunks of fruit in ice cream instead of just using the fruit juice to give it flavor. In the early 1990s, people took this idea to the extreme! Ice cream companies began putting unusual ingredients in ice cream, like chunks of fudge, swirls of caramel, marshmallows, and even chocolate chip cookie dough!

More recently, ice cream shops started mixing ingredients in the ice cream right in front of the customers. You pick your flavor of ice cream. Then you pick what you want in it. There are many options, such as candy bar bits, gummy candy, nuts, or cookies. They put it on a flat board and mix it together with spatulas! Then they put it in a bowl or in a cone. Joey Monticello, a seven-year-old in Michigan, loves to go to his favorite ice cream shop that does this. His dad usually gets chocolate ice cream mixed with chocolate chips, chocolate sauce, and a brownie. His mom often gets plain chocolate ice cream, but if she wants to splurge, she has it mixed with a brownie and caramel sauce. Joey always starts with chocolate ice cream, but he has a hard time deciding between having it mixed with gummy bears or sprinkles.

The newest ice cream trend is ice cream beads! Ice cream comes in little tiny balls. You can roll them around in your bowl before you eat them. They will eventually melt, but they melt a lot slower than other kinds of ice cream. Of course, it's impossible to put them on a cone! The ice cream beads come in traditional and unusual flavors.

What's next? Who knows…maybe you'll invent the next ice cream fad!

Answer the questions below.

1. What two ingredients are in an ice cream soda?

_____

2. When were ice cream sodas popular?

_____

3. In what two forms can fruit be in ice cream?

_____

4. When did companies start putting unusual ingredients in ice cream?

_____

5. What word in paragraph 3 means the same as *choices*?

_____

6. What kind of ice cream does Joey get?

_____

7. What two items does he decide between to have it mixed with?

_____

8. What would melt faster, an ice cream sundae or ice cream beads?

_____

9. Do ice cream beads come in one flavor or more than one flavor?

_____

10. What word in the last sentence means the same as *trend*?

_____

The Tripper and the Double Dipper

Isabel and Victoria are sisters. They have a lot of the same interests. They both like to skate, like to text message their friends, and love ice cream! Isabel's favorite ice cream is chocolate banana crunch, and Victoria's favorite is fudge frenzy. Every summer, their parents buy gallons of ice cream, and they get to have it once a week. They even have their own ice cream scoops. Isabel has a blue scoop because blue is her favorite color, and Victoria has a yellow scoop for the same reason.

Last summer, Victoria and Isabel went skating in the park one Monday. While they were skating, Victoria got a text message from her friend Marvin. She reached in her pocket and read the message. While she was reading it, she tripped on her skates and fell. Isabel immediately used her cell phone to call for help. Victoria's parents came, and everyone went to the hospital. The doctor took X-rays, and told Victoria she broke her arm.

When they got home, their parents said they could have ice cream. Isabel scooped up ice cream for both of them since Victoria's arm was in a cast. Because Victoria had a broken arm, their parents said they could have ice cream every day for a month. They were so excited. Isabel scooped ice cream every day for a week. She scooped three scoops of chocolate banana crunch for her and three scoops of fudge frenzy for Victoria. She did the same the second week. By the third week, she was very tired of scooping ice cream for two! She thought her arm was going to break if she had to keep scooping so much ice cream.

She decided to take the ice cream scoops and tape them together. She taped her blue scoop to Victoria's yellow scoop. Then she put the gallons of ice cream next to each other and two bowls next to each other. She grabbed the scoop in the middle and scooped out two scoops at once—one with her favorite ice cream and one with her sister's favorite ice cream. Then she released the ice cream into two bowls. It was so much fun and half the work! She called her invention the Double Dipper.

She liked the invention so much that she kept it when Victoria's arm got better. They took turns using the Double Dipper, but they only had ice cream once a week.

Read each statement. Check whether it is true for either *Isabel* or *Victoria*.
Sometimes both are possible.

	Isabel	Victoria
1. Her favorite ice cream is chocolate banana crunch.		
2. Her favorite ice cream is fudge frenzy.		
3. Her favorite color is yellow.		
4. She has a blue ice cream scoop.		
5. She got a text message from Marvin.		
6. She fell and broke her arm.		
7. She called her parents.		
8. She went to the hospital.		
9. She invented the Double Dipper.		
10. She used the Double Dipper.		

Slower Than Slow

Try walking in a line while you count to 60. How many feet did you walk? You probably walked at least 100 feet in a minute. A sloth, one of the slowest animals in the world, moves 5 feet in one minute. If it is in danger it can go faster—15 feet per minute! The word *sloth* actually means "lazy". However, sloths aren't lazy. They move slowly to protect themselves. Eagles are enemies of the sloth, and eagles hunt by seeing something move. Since the sloths move so slowly, eagles often don't even know they're nearby! As you can imagine, a sloth would have trouble catching fast animals. It eats mostly slow-moving insects that live in trees, and it eats leaves.

Another slow animal is the giant tortoise. It's only a little bit faster than the sloth. It usually moves about 15 feet per minute. Tortoises protect themselves from their enemies with their giant hard shells. Another slow animal with a hard shell is the garden snail. Garden snails are very slow. They're even slower than sloths. Of course, they are also a lot smaller. They move about 2.5 feet in one minute! It could take them an entire day to walk across a garden!

Are there living things slower than a snail? Yes, there are. There are some living things that don't move at all! You may have heard of coral, but did you know it is actually a marine animal? Corals live in the ocean on the ocean floor. They live in shallow water because they need sunlight. They don't move at all. They eat very small living organisms that float by them.

You may have a sponge in your house that you use to do the dishes, but did you know that sponges are also living things? Not the sponges you use at home, but sponges found in the ocean. They also live on the ocean floor, and they are very slow. They are like the corals because they don't move at all! They can eat their food by pumping water through their bodies and taking out any tiny pieces of food in the water.

So, if anyone ever tells you that you move as slowly as a turtle, you can say that's pretty fast compared to corals and sponges!

Read each question. Circle the correct answer.

1. What is the main topic of the reading?
   a. the sloth
   b. slow animals
   c. ocean animals

2. What is the main idea of paragraph 1?
   a. Sloths are slow.
   b. Sloths are lazy.
   c. Sloths eat leaves.

3. What word in paragraph 1 is the opposite of *fast*?
   a. slow
   b. slower
   c. slowest

4. What word in paragraph 2 is the opposite of *slower*?
   a. smaller
   b. harder
   c. faster

5. How fast does a giant tortoise move?
   a. $2\frac{1}{2}$ feet per minute
   b. 5 feet per minute
   c. 15 feet per minute

6. What is paragraph 2 about?
   a. two animals slower than sloths
   b. giants tortoises and garden snails
   c. gardens

7. What two animals don't move at all?
   a. sloths and giant tortoises
   b. corals and sponges
   c. garden snails and corals

8. What does *marine* mean in paragraph 3?
   a. living in the ocean
   b. very slow
   c. not moving

9. What is a sponge?
   a. something used to clean dishes
   b. a marine animal
   c. both a and b

10. What is the purpose of the last paragraph?
   a. to make you laugh
   b. to give you information about turtles
   c. to tell you that you're slow

Okapi: A Zebra-Horse-Giraffe?

The okapi is an unusual animal with an unusual name. It's pronounced *oh-kah-pee*. Okapis have reddish-brown colored hair that is similar to a horse's in texture. Their legs have black and white stripes, which make them look like zebras. Scientists think the stripes on the legs help young okapis see their mothers in the dark forest. They walk behind their mothers and follow the bright white stripes on their legs. However, okapis are actually relatives of the giraffe. Sometimes they are called forest giraffes. Okapis are almost the same shape as a giraffe, but they have much shorter necks.

They might have short necks, but okapis have very long tongues! Their tongues are blue, and they're almost ten inches long. They are long so okapis can reach leaves on tree branches. Okapis take the leaves off the trees and eat them. They also eat grass and fruit. When they're done eating, okapis clean themselves with their tongues. Their tongues are so long that they can even clean their own eyelids and ears with them! Okapis have very large ears. They are large to help them hear their enemies. Their biggest enemy is the leopard.

Adult okapis are about 8 feet long and 6.5 feet tall. Their tails are between 12 and 17 inches long. They can weigh 450 to 550 pounds! Scientists think they live about 30 years. There is still a lot to learn about okapis. They are not seen very often in the wild.

Okapis live in only one country in the entire world. They live in the rainforest in the Democratic Republic of Congo. It is in central Africa. People living in the rainforest have known about them for a long time, but other people didn't know they existed until 1901! In 1937, an okapi came to the Bronx Zoo in New York City. It was the first okapi ever in North America.

Okapis are awake during the day, and they sleep at night. Okapis are solitary animals. In fact, they are alone most of the time. However, baby okapis stay with their mothers until they're adults. If you see two okapi together, you can be pretty sure that they are mother and child! But it's very unlikely you'll see even one okapi unless you go to a zoo. They are very good at hiding in the rainforest.

Complete the chart with information from the reading.

Okapi Facts

1. Height	
2. Length	
3. Weight	
4. Animals they look like	
5. What they eat	
6. Their enemy	

Match each word to its defintion. Write the letter on the line.

7. _____ entire

8. _____ solitary

9. _____ existed

10. _____ central

a. lived

b. whole

c. like to be alone

d. in the middle

Kendra and the Eucalyptus Leaves

Koala bears live in Australia in the Outback, which is a very large desert. They are vegetarians. That means that they don't eat meat. Koala bears eat mainly eucalyptus leaves. Eucalyptus leaves grow on eucalyptus trees all over in the Outback. The leaves taste good, and they smell wonderful, too. Koala bears have eaten them for years and years. That is, until Kendra the Koala was born.

Kendra the Koala is a joey. No, her name isn't Joey, she *is* a joey! A joey is a baby koala bear. Kendra lived in her mother's pouch for seven months and drank milk. Koala bears have pouches just like kangaroos! Then she rode on her mother's back for six months. Now she is a year old, and she is ready to explore the world.

Her mother is showing her how to be a koala bear. She says that koalas sleep about twenty hours a day. They are only awake for about four hours. During the four hours, they spend two of them eating. They sleep during the day, and they eat at night. Kendra's mother takes her to a nice eucalyptus tree one night. They climb up, and Kendra's mom starts eating. She tears off the leaf with her fingers and thumb. Koalas have thumbs, and they even have thumbprints and fingerprints! Kendra's mom shows her how to tear the leaves, and Kendra puts one in her mouth. Kendra doesn't like the eucalyptus leaf. She says, "Mom, I don't like this."

Mom says, "But you have to like it. All koalas like eucalyptus leaves."

"Not me!" says Kendra. "Let's find something else to eat."

Kendra and her mom search for something else to eat. Kendra tries grass. Her mom says, "You can't eat grass. Kangaroos eat grass."

"That's OK, Mom. I don't like grass either. Let's find something else." They pass a river and see a fish jumping out of it. "What's that?" asks Kendra.

"It's a fish, but you can't eat fish. Fish are for crocodiles," says Mom.

"What's a crocodile?" asks Kendra as a large, scary crocodile pulls its head out of the water and snaps at a fish.

"That's a crocodile," says Mom.

"Oh," whispers Kendra, clinging to her mother's back. "You know what, Mom. I don't want to try fish. I decided I like eucalyptus leaves!"

Complete each sentence. Use the words in the word bank. Use each word two times.

pouch   Outback   crocodile   vegetarian   joey

1. Kendra is a _____.

2. Kendra and her mom live in the _____.

3. A _____ doesn't eat meat.

4. _____ is a boy's name.

5. Kendra's mom is a _____.

6. Kendra's mother has a _____.

7. A _____ eats fish.

8. The _____ is a desert in Australia.

9. A kangaroo has a _____.

10. A _____ scared Kendra.

Roller Coaster Craze

Roller coasters are popular rides at amusement parks around the world. A roller coaster always has a track that is like a railroad track, except it doesn't go in a straight line on the ground. Roller coaster tracks go up and down hills, and they even turn in loops. Cars with wheels ride on the tracks. Two, four, or six people sit in each car. Several cars are hooked together and go on the tracks at the same time. Roller coasters can be made out of wood or steel. Metal roller coasters are more popular today, but many people like the older wooden roller coasters because of the bumpy ride.

The idea of roller coasters came from winter sled rides in Russia in the seventeenth century. People made special hills from snow and ice for the sleds. Some of the hills were as tall as 80 feet. The rides were so popular that people began to copy them. They started to use tracks and cars instead of snow and sleds. The first roller coaster on tracks was in Paris, France.

The first roller coaster in the United States was in Pennsylvania in 1827. It was *Gravity Road*. It used to be a track for delivering coal in a mine, and it was turned into a ride for people. It cost 50 cents to ride it. Roller coasters became very popular and were in amusement parks all over the world. They remained popular in the United States until the Great Depression in the 1930s. Many people could hardly afford food for their families, so they definitely could not afford amusement parks. In the 1970s roller coasters became popular again, and they continue to be popular today.

Amusement parks have their name because people go to them to be amused, or entertained. People have many emotions when they ride roller coasters. Some people are nervous and scared. Others are excited and happy. Some people have mixed emotions. At first they are nervous and scared, but after the ride they are happy and excited and want to ride it again!

Complete each sentence. Circle the correct word in the parentheses.

1. Two, four, or six people can sit in each (track / car) in a roller coaster.

2. Roller coasters can be made out of wood or (metal / loops).

3. The idea for the first roller coaster came from sled rides in (France / Russia).

4. The first roller coaster on tracks was in (Paris / Pennsylvania).

5. The first roller coaster in the United States cost (80 / 50) cents to ride.

6. The track on *Gravity Road* used to be for delivering (coal / steel).

7. Roller coasters were not popular in the (1930s / 1970s).

8. People who ride roller coasters have (the same / different) emotions.

9. Amusement parks got their name because the rides (scare / amuse) people.

10. The main topic of this reading is (amusement parks / roller coasters).

Amusement for Everyone

Cedar Point is a large and popular amusement park in Ohio. It has something for everyone, and not just roller coasters!

Rides

Of course, Cedar Point does have roller coasters. In fact, it has seventeen of them. *Mean Streak* is one of its famous wooden roller coasters. It is 161 feet tall and goes 65 miles per hour. The steel roller coaster, *Magnum XL-200*, goes even faster. It goes 72 miles per hour and has one hill that is 205 feet high. *Corkscrew* is a favorite because the cars and tracks go upside-down several times.

Cedar Point has many other kinds of rides for all ages. It has nine rides called *thrill rides* that are fast and exciting. The *Demon Drop* plunges 131 feet in 6 seconds! There are six spinning rides. On *Wave Swinger,* you sit high up in swings that spin around in a large circle. There are eight tranquil rides for people who don't like as much speed and thrills. For example, you can ride around in antique cars. There are also three carousels, 23 rides for very young children, and two water rides. If you really like water, you can go to Soak City, which is another park with only water rides. Soak City is connected to Cedar Point, but you have to pay a separate entrance fee.

Cost

It's not cheap to go to Cedar Point, but there are discounts for seniors and children. It costs $41.95 for anyone between the ages of 3 and 61. Children under two years old are free. If you are between two and three years old or under 48 inches tall, it's only $11.95. This is because you have to be at least 48 inches to ride many of the rides. If you're 62 or older, it also costs $11.95. Pets aren't allowed, but there is is a Pet Check where you can leave your dog or cat for the day!

Other Attractions

You don't just get the rides for your money. There are a lot of other things to do at Cedar Point. There are many shows with music, dancing, and even ice-skating. There is a museum, and there's a petting farm, too. There's even a beach because Cedar Point is near Lake Erie. Cedar Point has many restaurants, but if you don't want to spend time sitting down to eat, you can buy a quick snack at a food stand in the park.

Match each fact from the reading to its number. Write the letter on the line.

1. _____ How long it takes to go down *Demon Drop*

2. _____ Height of one hill on *Magnum XL-200*

3. _____ Cost to enter Cedar Point if you're older than 61

4. _____ Number of roller coasters at Cedar Point

5. _____ Number of rides for little children at Cedar Point

6. _____ Speed of *Mean Streak*

7. _____ Speed of *Magnum XL-200*

8. _____ Height of *Mean Streak*

9. _____ How tall you must be to ride many of the rides at Cedar Point

10. _____ Cost to enter Cedar Point if you're between the ages of 3 and 61

a. 161 feet

b. 205 feet

c. 65 mph

d. 72 mph

e. 17

f. 23

g. 6 seconds

h. $41.95

i. $11.95

j. 48 inches

Ups and Downs with Donut

Dorothy and Doug Donovan's grandparents picked them up one Saturday to take them to an amusement park. Dorothy and Doug said, "Bye, Mom and Dad. Don't forget to feed Donut!"

"We won't," said Dad. "Have fun!"

Donut is Doug and Dorothy's pet rabbit. She's extremely sneaky. In fact, Donut snuck into their grandparents' car when no one was looking. When they got to the park, Donut hopped out and ran off.

"Look!" said Dorothy. "It's Donut. Oh, no!"

"Don't worry," said Grandma as she paid the entrance fee for two children and two seniors. "We'll find her."

Donut hopped in the front car on the *Speedy Bullet*—a fast and thrilling roller coaster. Dorothy, Doug, Grandpa, and Grandma got on the ride, too. They were scared, but they also thought it was fun as they went down the big, steel hills. When they got off the ride, Donut hopped away faster than a speedy bullet.

She hopped into the *Mad Castle* funhouse. Dorothy and Doug followed her while Grandma and Grandpa waited outside. It was hard to find Donut because the floors were slanted, and there were silly mirrors everywhere. Finally, they saw Donut hop toward the exit, and they ran after her. Then they all followed her into a theater and watched Donut hop to an empty seat in front. The show had already started, so an usher made Doug, Dorothy, and their grandparents sit in back so they wouldn't interrupt. He didn't see Donut. They all watched an ice-skating show called *Iguanas on Ice.* It was very funny to see people dressed up as iguanas skating to music!

After the show, Donut hopped out of the theater quickly and got on a carousel. Everyone followed her. Dorothy rode on a carousel horse, and Doug was on a carousel grasshopper.Grandma was on a ladybug, and Grandpa rode a zebra. Donut was on a rabbit, which made everyone laugh.

They chased Donut for two more hours riding on all kinds of exciting rides before they finally gave up and sat down.They decided it had been a great day. After all, they went on rides they might have been too scared to ride had Donut not hopped on them first! Just then, Donut hopped on Doug's lap and fell asleep. Grandpa pointed to a sign behind them and said, "Look, you can check your pets for the day while you ride the rides!" Everyone laughed hysterically, and Donut snored loudly.

Number the events in the correct order. The events are not told in the story, but you can figure out when they would have happened based on the other events in the story.

_____ Doug, Dorothy, Grandma, and Grandpa sit down and eat ice cream.

_____ Grandpa drives to the amusement park.

_____ Dorothy and Doug tell their parents about their amusing day.

_____ A woman makes sure Dorothy is tall enough to ride the carousel.

_____ Grandpa and Grandma take Dorothy and Doug home.

_____ Donut hides in the backseat of Grandma and Grandpa's car.

_____ Everyone claps when *Iguanas on Ice* ends.

_____ Grandma and Doug scream on the *Speedy Bullet*.

_____ Grandpa points to a sign that says *Pet Palace*.

_____ Grandpa and Grandma help someone with directions while Doug and Dorothy are in the *Mad Castle*.

It Pays to Save

Kristin Twichell lives in the Michigan countryside with her parents and her brother. Her mother has a very good friend named Kate who lives in New York City. Kate visits Michigan every year and is like an aunt to Kristin. When Kristin was in third grade, she decided she wanted to visit Kate in New York City. Her mom said, "Maybe when you're older." When Kristin was in fourth grade, she still wanted to visit Kate in the big city. Her mom said, "Maybe when you're older." When Kristin was in fifth grade, her mom said, "OK. We can visit Kate in New York City."

Her mom decided Kristin should save money for half of her plane ticket. Her mom would pay for the other half and give her spending money. Her mom thought this would be a good way for Kristin to learn about saving money. She also thought it would take her over a year, so that she would be even older before they went on the trip.

That year for Christmas, Kristin asked for money instead of gifts. She did the same for her birthday. By spring, Kristin had enough money for half of a plane ticket. She told her mom, who was very surprised! She thought it would take Kristin a lot longer to save the money. She was very proud of Kristin. There was only one problem. Her mom didn't have the money for her part of the trip! She decided that since Kristin had sacrificed presents to save for the trip, she better get the money fast. She started to save, too, and they planned a trip to New York City for the summer.

Kristin had a fabulous time in the city. Kristin had two things she really wanted to do. She wanted to see a play on Broadway and have a cappuccino in a coffee house. She saw movies of people drinking cappuccinos in coffee houses in New York City and thought it would be fun. They went to a coffee house, but Kristin decided she didn't like cappuccino! She liked everything else about New York though. They went shopping, went to Central Park, and went to museums. Her favorite part was the Broadway play.

At the end of the trip, she decided that she liked living in the country more, but she does want to visit New York again. She also learned that it's fun to save money and use it for something you've always wanted to do!

Complete each sentence. Use the words in the word bank. Then write whether the statement is a *fact* or an *opinion*.

> fifth   surprised   cappuccino   museums   country
>
> money   plane   New York City   visit   play

_____ **1.** New York City was a fun place to _____.

_____ **2.** I was in _____ grade when Mom said I could go to New York.

_____ **3.** I saved money for half of my _____ ticket.

_____ **4.** Saving _____ is important.

_____ **5.** My mom was _____ that I saved money so fast.

_____ **6.** _____ doesn't taste good.

_____ **7.** There are a lot of _____ in New York.

_____ **8.** The Broadway _____ was fabulous!

_____ **9.** Living in the _____ is better than living in the city.

_____ **10.** I want to go to _____ again.

A Trip for Two

Fifth graders can experience life in another country. Our program lets students from the United States and Mexico see what it is like to live in each other's country. You will stay with a host family for a month. Read about what life will be like in your "new" country.

	Mexico	The United States
Family stay	You will stay with a family in Mexico City. There are almost 9 million people living in Mexico City.	You will stay with a family in Chicago. There are almost 3 million people living in Chicago.
Meals	You will have a large breakfast at 6:00 AM. You will also have a big lunch at home at 2:00 PM. At 8:00 PM, you will have a small snack.	You will have a small breakfast at 7:30 AM. You will have lunch at school at 12:30 PM. You will have dinner at home at 6:00 PM.
School	You will go to school from 7:00 AM to 1:00 PM.	You will go to school from 8:30 AM to 2:30 PM.
After school	Mexican students usually go back to school after they have lunch at home to take English classes. You will go back to school at 3:30 PM for extra classes to help you learn Spanish. You will also do fun projects to learn more about Mexico.	American students often have practice for sports right after school. You will go to classes to help you learn more English at this time. Classes start at 3:00 PM. You will also play fun games with American students on some days.
Outings	You will visit the National Museum of Anthropology, the Zocalo, and Xochimilco. The Zocalo is a neighborhood with a big plaza and lots of shopping. Xochimilco has floating gardens and ancient ruins.	You will visit the Museum of Science and Industry, Wrigley Field, and the John Hancock Center. You will see a baseball game at Wrigley Field. You will go to the top floor of the Hancock Center and see great views of the city.
Weekend get-away	One weekend, you will go with your host family to the beach in Acapulco.	One weekend, you will go with your host family to the Six Flags amusement park.
Party	There will be a big fiesta on your last day. You will eat traditional Mexican food and hear salsa music.	There will be a party on your last day. You will eat hotdogs and hamburgers and listen to a blues band.

Read each statement. Write *true* or *false*.

1. More people live in Mexico City than in Chicago.

_____

2. The students in Mexico City will eat breakfast later than the students in Chicago.

_____

3. The students in Chicago will eat a bigger meal at night than the students in Mexico City.

_____

4. The students in Chicago will have a longer school day than the students in Mexico City.

_____

5. The students in Chicago and the students in Mexico City will have after school activities.

_____

6. The students in Chicago and the students in Mexico City will eat lunch at school.

_____

7. The students in Mexico City and the students in Chicago will visit museums.

_____

8. The students in Mexico City will go shopping, and the students in Chicago will go to a sporting event.

_____

9. Students in Chicago and Mexico City will not have a weekend trip.

_____

10. There will be music at the parties in Mexico City and Chicago.

_____

Cooking Trip

1 My father's a chef and he has a knack
2 For making desserts and delicious snacks
3 Chocolate tortes and pecan pies
4 Homemade ice cream, even French fries

5 One day he created a special treat
6 A delicious cake that was sour and sweet
7 It had layers of lemons and layers of jam
8 He called it *Lemony-jamony-yumony-slam*

9 I tried it and said, "What a surprise!
10 This is delicious. It should win a prize!"
11 That gave him an idea and he started to dance
12 He told me about a cooking contest in France

13 "Julie, pack your bags! Get your coat! Hurry, I say.
14 We're going to France, and we're leaving today."
15 I ran upstairs and screamed to my mom,
16 "We're going to France. Come on! Come on!"

17 Dad packed bowls and pans and a big mixing spoon
18 He said, "Come on! Come on! We're leaving soon!"
19 Mom and I packed faster than ever before
20 Then we all took our suitcases and ran out the door

21 We got to France just in time
22 For Dad to get in the entry line
23 He cooked for hours with other chefs
24 Then we found out who was best

25 First prize went to Miss Jennifer Lake
26 A woman from Canada who knows how to bake
27 And my dad, you wonder, "How did he do?"
28 *Lemony-jamony-yumony-slam* came in number two!

Read each question. Circle the correct answer.

1. What can you infer that a *torte* is in line 3?
   a. a baking pan
   b. a cook
   c. a dessert

2. What is *lemony-jamony-yumony-slam*?
   a. the name of a famous chef
   b. the name of a dessert
   c. the name of a country

3. What words are opposites in lines 5–8?
   a. sour and sweet
   b. lemons and layers
   c. treat and sweet

4. What does Julie think of her dad's cake?
   a. She thinks it's sour.
   b. She thinks it's sweet.
   c. She thinks it tastes good.

5. Why does Julie's dad dance?
   a. because he won a prize
   b. because Julie likes his cake
   c. because he has a good idea

6. Where is Julie going with her parents?
   a. to Canada
   b. to France
   c. home

7. When does Julie's family get to the cooking contest?
   a. in time for her dad to enter the contest
   b. the day after her dad made the cake
   c. two days before the contest

8. Who won first place in the contest?
   a. Julie's dad
   b. a woman from France
   c. a woman from Canada

9. From whose perspective is the poem told?
   a. the father's
   b. the daughter's
   c. the son's

10. What is the mood of the poem?
   a. serious and sad
   b. special and delicious
   c. happy and humorous

Get Around Town

How do you get to school? What kinds of transportation do you take on vacation? What's the most unusual vehicle you've ridden in? There are many different ways to get around. Some are common and others are unique.

Road and Rail

Vehicles that travel on the road have wheels. The most common are cars, trucks, vans, and buses. In some cities, people pay drivers to take them places. Taxis are the most common form of this type of transportation. Rickshaws are not as common, but they exist in some places. A rickshaw is a carriage on two wheels that someone pulls by walking, or sometimes it's attached to a bike. Bikes, motorbikes, skates, and scooters are other ways to get around on wheels. Today, tennis shoes with wheels in the heels are even popular!

Subways and trains run on tracks. Subways are great for getting around in cities. A train is a great mode of transportation when you travel long distances.

Water

Some vehicles float and move on water. Many of these vehicles have motors, like boats and ships. Some move by sails and others by manpower. Kayaks and rowboats are popular man-powered water vehicles, but they're usually used for pleasure, not for getting from one place to another. Submarines are water vehicles that travel underwater.

Air and Space

Aircrafts include planes, jets, and helicopters.

People often travel on large jets to get to places that are far away. They may travel on small planes to get to places that aren't as far away. People usually only travel on helicopters to get to remote places, or they may take a helicopter ride for fun! People also take hot air balloon rides for fun.

Space travel isn't yet available to everyone. Astronauts are scientists trained to travel in space. In the past, astronauts have traveled to the moon, and they still travel by shuttle to get the International Space Station.

Cable cars run on cable wire to get people from place to place. This is sometimes done in cities, and some places like big zoos have cable cars going from one end to the other. The most common cable cars are ski lifts. They get you from the bottom of the mountain to the top!

Do you get around by road, rail, water, or air? The most economical way to get around is by walking! You don't need a vehicle for that; *you* are the vehicle!

Read each question. Circle the correct answer.

1. What is the main idea of the reading?
   a. getting to work
   b. ways to get around
   c. water transportation

2. What is the main topic in paragraph 4?
   a. road vehicles
   b. aircraft
   c. water transportation

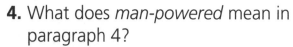

3. What does *economical* mean in the last paragraph?
   a. doesn't have wheels
   b. isn't a vehicle
   c. not expensive

4. What does *man-powered* mean in paragraph 4?
   a. humans provide the force to make it move
   b. men can drive it, but women can't
   c. it only works on water

5. Which item is **not** part of a rickshaw?
   a. wheels
   b. a motor
   c. a carriage

6. Which item is **not** an aircraft?
   a. a jet
   b. a helicopter
   c. a scooter

7. What does *remote* mean in paragraph 5?
   a. hard to get to
   b. close by
   c. fun

8. What is the topic of paragraph 7?
   a. air travel
   b. cable cars
   c. space shuttles

9. Which detail supports the topic Road and Rail?
   a. Some vehicles float and move on water.
   b. Bikes, motorbikes, skates, and scooters are other ways to get around on wheels.
   c. People often travel on jets to get places that are far away.

10. What is the purpose of this reading?
    a. to tell you how to get to school
    b. to tell you about different kinds of transportation
    c. to encourage you to walk everywhere

Bicycles, Bikes, and Cycles

"Let's go for a bike ride" is something you might say when you want to ride a bike with your friends for fun. A lot of people use bicycles for recreation, but there are many other uses for bicycles.

Many people use bicycles for transportation. They may take them to work instead of cars or buses. This is especially popular in big cities in some countries, such as China. It's a very cheap way to travel. Other people use bikes for their jobs. Some people deliver packages or small bags of groceries on bikes. In some places, people even deliver pizzas on bikes. Some may even deliver people! In some cities people ride bikes while pulling rickshaws to help people get from one place to another. Of course, bikes break down, so some people have jobs repairing them.

Bicycling is a good form of exercise, so a lot of people bike to stay in shape. Some people ride in bike-a-thons to raise money. They ask people to pledge money for each mile they will ride. Then, when the bike-a-thon is over, they collect the money for how many miles they were able to go. The money goes to a charity. Other bikers compete in races. The most famous bicycle competition is the Tour de France. Lance Armstrong is a famous cyclist who won the race seven times! When people ride bicycles as a sport, they are usually called cyclists.

Some people collect vintage bikes because they may be worth a lot of money. The first bikes were called pushbikes, and they didn't have pedals. You sat on the seat and pushed with your feet on the ground to make the wheels move. There is a bicycle museum in Ohio where you can see many antique bikes as well as modern ones.

Bicycles have even been used in art. Marcel Duchamp made a famous sculpture of a bike wheel. Leonardo da Vinci drew a famous sketch of a bicycle. One of the most unusual uses of a bike was to make music! In 1963, musician Frank Zappa actually played a bicycle on a TV show.

Read each statement. Write the reason each person uses a bicycle. Use the words in the word bank. Some words will be used more than once.

recreation   transportation   work   exercise

competition   collection   art

1. Michael rides his bike to soccer practice every week.

_____

2. Jenny came in first place in Bike Boston last week.

_____

3. Rick and his dad went on a short bike ride in the park.

_____

4. Martin rides a bike in place for 30 minutes every day.

_____

5. Elsa has a bike from 1924. She never rides it.

_____

6. Joan made a sculpture of a bicycle out of clay.

_____

7. Kelly delivered three pizzas on his bike Tuesday night.

_____

8. Mr. Garcia rides his bike to the office every day.

_____

9. Todd cycled 40 miles in his last race.

_____

10. It took Ali 30 minutes to ride his bike to OfficeWeb to deliver the package.

_____

The Bike Share

Mario, Lekisha, Dan, and Carla live on the same block, are in the same class, and are good friends. They all want bicycles, but they don't have enough money. Mario has a great idea. He says, "I think we should buy one bike. We can share it!"

"That's a great idea," say Dan, Lekisha, and Carla.

They save their money for a couple of months. Then they buy a shiny, red bicycle. They work out a schedule for the weekends. On Saturday morning, Lekisha takes the bike to the park to exercise. When she gets home, she drops it off at Dan's house. Dan takes the bike to soccer practice because his parents work in the morning. Carla's mom takes her to swimming lessons in the afternoon. The pool is close to the soccer field, so Carla's mom takes Dan home, and they leave the bike for Carla.

Carla rides the bike home after swimming lessons, and she leaves it at Mario's house. Mario rides the bike for fun around the neighborhood before it gets dark. The plan goes really well for a month. Then Carla has an idea. She says, "I think we should take turns using the bike on other days to make money!"

"That's a great idea!" say Dan, Lekisha, and Mario. On Sundays, Dan uses the bike to get groceries for his neighbor Mrs. Jones. She gives him a few dollars as a tip every time. Lekisha uses the bike for a paper route. Some evenings, Carla takes the bike to baby-sit twins who live on the other side of town. On Saturdays, Mario decides to deliver advertisements for his mom's company instead of riding around the neighborhood for fun.

In a month, they get together and count their money. Lekisha has an incredible idea. She says, "We can buy another bike! That way, we can each ride twice as much."

Dan says, "Yes! In another month, we can buy a third bike. The month after that, we can buy a fourth bike! Then we'll each have a bike."

"That's a great idea," say Carla and Mario.

Their plan works, and in a few months, they each have a bike. They bought the exact same bike three more times, so they wouldn't fight over who got the new bike. Now every weekend, they ride their identical bikes to the park together!

Check the correct person for each activity. Sometimes more than one person is possible.

	Dan	Mario	Lekisha	Carla
1. plays soccer				
2. has swimming lessons				
3. uses the bike for exercise				
4. delivers groceries				
5. gets a ride from Carla's mom				
6. delivers newspapers				
7. works for his mom				
8. has a red bike				
9. has a great idea				
10. has the idea to buy the first bike				

May 8, Any Year

Have you ever wondered how many important events happened on one specific date? Many important events happened on May 8th. Here are just a few of them.

Important Historical Events

On May 8, 1541, explorer Hernando de Soto reached the Mississippi River. On May 8, 1919, Australian Edward Honey said there should be a moment of silence for the end of World War I. This was the first time someone suggested this idea. Today, many people have a minute of silence at public events in memory of people who have died. On May 8 in 1933, Mohandas Gandhi began a 21-day food fast in India. A fast is when you don't eat for a period of time. He was protesting the mistreatment of people in his country. Forty years later, a 71-day standoff between the U.S. government and American Indians ended at Wounded Knee, South Dakota. The American Indians agreed to leave if the government helped with American Indian issues. In 1999, on the 8th of May, Nancy Mace graduated from the Citadel. It was an all-male military college before then.

Inventions

Some important inventions were created on May 8th. In 1886, Dr. John Pemberton invented a soft drink. He later named it Coca-Cola. In the same year as Gandhi's food fast, the first car radios were installed in police cars in New York City. Before this day, policemen were not able to have contact with police headquarters or with each other when driving.

Natural Disasters

Unfortunately, on any date, there has probably been a natural disaster in the world. On May 8, 1902, Mount Pelée erupted on the Caribbean Island of Martinique. The eruption killed over 30,000 people. In 1950, 23 people died in floods in Nebraska.

Birthdays and Holidays

Many famous people were born on May 8th. Some of them were historical figures, like Jean Dunant and Harry S. Truman. Dunant was born in 1828, and he founded the Red Cross. Truman was born 56 years later, and he was the 33rd president of the United States. Some are famous people who are still alive. Melissa Gilbert, from the television show *Little House on the Prairie*, was born on May 8, 1964. Eleven years later, singer Enrique Iglesias was born.

There are a few holidays on May 8th. World Red Cross Day is on this day. VE day, or Victory in Europe Day, celebrates the end of World War II. In South Korea, May 8th is Parents' Day.

Complete the timeline with the correct dates from the reading.

May 8...

An explorer gets to the Mississippi.

The founder of the Red Cross is born.

The 33rd president of the United States is born.

Coca-Cola is invented.

A volcano erupts and kills many people.

The first moment of silence is held.

Gandhi stops eating to protest.

Radios are put in police cars.

Floods kill people in Nebraska.

The argument at Wounded Knee ends.

Enrique Iglesias is born.

A woman graduated from the Citadel.

Predicting the Future

Have you ever had your palm read? Has anyone ever looked into a crystal ball and told you your future? These people are called fortunetellers, but there are many other jobs in which people predict the future.

Financial advisors study companies to find out which ones are going to make money. Then they advise their clients to buy stock in companies that may do well. When a person buys stock in a company, he or she is purchasing a very small piece of ownership in that business. When a company is successful, the value of its stock rises. Then people who own stock can make money by selling it at a higher price than they paid for it. Financial advisors who make accurate predictions can earn a lot of money for their clients by helping them buy stock in the best companies.

Pollsters are people who take opinion polls, or surveys, to predict the outcome of an event. For example, before an election, pollsters ask small groups of people in different parts of a country which candidate they will vote for. The answers from these small groups help predict how all of the people in the country might vote. Other times, a poll might ask people their opinions on a certain issue, such as taxes. This helps determine which candidate voters might choose. For example, if a poll shows that most people are against new taxes and Ms. Green is the candidate who opposes new taxes, it is sensible to predict that Ms. Green will win.

Some art collectors also try to predict the future. They buy art from unknown artists, guessing that the artists will one day become famous. If their predictions are correct, the collectors can make a lot of money by selling paintings or sculptures they paid very little for.

Meteorologists study the atmosphere to predict the weather. Weather forecasts are given on the news and on the Internet so that people can prepare for the following day or even for future vacations. Meteorologists forecast the weather by studying the temperature, air pressure, and water vapor in the earth's atmosphere. They can predict approximately what temperature it will be, and if it will be sunny, cloudy, windy, or rainy. They can even foresee storms such as tornados, thunderstorms, and hurricanes. Predicting the weather has gotten easier because of computers and satellites in space. Meteorology is extremely important. Accurate predictions can help people prepare for the future, and not just what clothing to pack for a vacation. For example, forecasts could help a farmer decide what crop to grow.

Fortunetellers are not the only people who can "see" the future!

Match each word to its synonym. Write the letter on the line. Use the context in the reading to help you.

1. _____ predict

2. _____ advise

3. _____ clients

4. _____ sensible

5. _____ outcome

6. _____ opinions

7. _____ well-known

8. _____ forecasts

9. _____ extremely

10. _____ accurate

a. predictions

b. customers

c. correct

d. views

e. recommend

f. result

g. famous

h. foresee

i. very

j. reasonable

Jeremy's Predictions

Jeremy Jiggins was curious about the future. He wondered what life would be like in the next 50 years. He decided to make several predictions. He wrote ten predictions for the future on a piece of paper. His predictions were:

By 2060…

• Scientists will discover a cure for many diseases, like cancer and diabetes. The cures will be painless and affordable.

• At least one woman will be president of the United States. There might even be as many as three female presidents by 2060.

• Wireless Internet connections will be available in every city and town. Computers will be much smaller, too. Some computers will fit in people's pockets.

• People will have small chips in their ears that are voice-activated phones. When someone calls them, they will just say, "Hello," and then be able to talk. The phones will be like earrings pierced to the top of people's ears.

• People will be able to ride in space shuttles to see space. Tickets will be very expensive, and only a few people will be able to go each month. There will be a long waiting list. People will have to have a medical exam first to make sure they are healthy enough to go.

• Everyone's DNA will be taken when they are born. All DNA will be entered into a computer system. This will help catch criminals in the future.

• Cars won't use gas anymore. Many cars will run on electricity. Someone will invent a car that runs on solar power, but the design won't be finished by 2060.

• Scientists will discover another planet. It will be farther away than Pluto, and they will see it with very powerful telescopes.

• There will be fewer poor people in the world because organizations and governments will find better ways to help them.

• Some food will be grown in huge skyscrapers instead of on farms. This will help the air because pesticides won't get into the air.

Jeremy put the piece of paper in a plastic bag, put the plastic bag in a metal box, and buried the metal box in his backyard. He decided he would dig it up in the year 2060 and see if any of his predictions came true. Do you think his predictions will come true? What are your predictions for the future?

Read each question. Circle the correct answer.

1. How old will Jeremy be in 2060?
   a. 10
   b. 50
   c. not enough information

2. How many predictions did Jeremy make?
   a. 10
   b. 50
   c. 60

3. According to Jeremy's prediction, how many diseases will scientists discover cures for?
   a. 2
   b. 10
   c. not enough information

4. How many female presidents does Jeremy think there will be in the US by 2060?
   a. only 1
   b. 1–3
   c. 0

5. What does *voice-activated* mean in Jeremy's fourth prediction?
   a. They are very small.
   b. They are in your ear.
   c. They work by using your voice.

6. What can you infer from Jeremy's prediction about space trips?
   a. Many people will take them.
   b. Only rich people will take them.
   c. Only scientists will take them.

7. According to Jeremy's prediction, what will DNA be used for?
   a. finding criminals
   b. allowing people to visit space
   c. curing diseases

8. What does *powerful* mean in Jeremy's eighth prediction?
   a. They can lift heavy objects.
   b. They allow scientists to see very far.
   c. They predict the future.

9. What can you infer from Jeremy's last prediction?
   a. Food grown in skyscrapers will taste better.
   b. Food grown in skyscrapers won't have any pesticides on them.
   c. Pesticides are bad for the environment.

10. What is the purpose of the author's last two questions?
   a. to give the reader a homework assignment
   b. to make the reader worry about the future
   c. to make the reader think about predictions for the future

How's It Going to End?

Many people judge movies by how good the ending is. There are different types of movie endings.

The Cliffhanger

Imagine a scene in a movie where a person is holding on to the edge of a cliff. All of a sudden, the movie ends. You don't know if the person falls off the cliff or is able to climb back up to safety. This is a cliffhanger ending. Of course, a movie can have a cliffhanger ending that doesn't actually end with someone on a cliff. It's an ending in which we have to imagine what happens after the movie ends. For example, a thriller might end when the hero solves one mystery, but is presented with a new mystery to solve. Many movies with cliffhanger endings have sequels. The cliffhanger ending makes you want to go and watch the next movie in the series.

Surprise Endings

Some movies make you think they are going to end a certain way. Suddenly, the movie ends in a way you weren't expecting. For example, maybe a character seems like he or she is going to die, but suddenly there is a miracle and the character lives! After the movie, you might think about what you saw to see if there were clues to the surprise ending you didn't notice.

Hollywood Endings

A Hollywood ending is a movie that ends happily. In Hollywood endings, all questions are usually answered, and all problems are solved. Imagine a movie where a father is looking for his long-lost son. In a movie with a Hollywood ending, the father and the son are reunited and live happily ever after.

Spoiler Alert!

A spoiler is when the ending of a movie is given before you see it. It's called a spoiler because it may spoil or ruin the movie for someone who hasn't seen it. An actor may accidentally reveal the ending of the movie in an interview. A movie reviewer may write about the ending of a movie in a magazine or online. Imagine you are going to see a new movie and your friend has already seen it. Your friend is telling you how good the movie is and tells you what happens at the end. Many people don't like to know the endings of movies before they see them.

Read each movie review. Write the kind of ending for each movie. Use the words in the word bank.

| Cliffhanger | Surprise Ending | Hollywood Ending |

1. Captain Mania finds an ancient treasure map. He searches an island for the buried treasure. He has a few accidents along the way. He eventually finds the treasure and shares it with his friends.

_____

2. Pauline and her twin sister were separated when they were born. Pauline and her friend Janice search for Pauline's sister. It turns out that Janice is actually Pauline's twin sister.

_____

3. Luke and Amy are stranded on an island. They live for a few years growing their own food and building a home. At the end, they talk about an idea for building a boat so they can leave.

_____

Answer the questions below.

4. In paragraph 1, what word means the same as *evaluate*? _____

5. In paragraph 2, what word means the same as *side*? _____

6. In paragraph 2, what word means the same as *figure out*?

_____

7. In paragraph 3, what word means the same as *thinking of*?

_____

8. In paragraph 4, what word means the same as *brought back together*?

_____

9. In paragraph 5, what word means the same as *ruin*? _____

10. In paragraph 5, what word means the same as *tell*? _____

It's Never Going to End!

"Lollipop, lollipop, oh, lolli, lolli, lolli, lollipop, lollipop!" are words to a famous song from the 1950s, but lollipops were invented many years earlier. However, it's a guessing game as to exactly when they were invented.

Lollipops, or suckers, are hard candy on a stick. They are usually made from sugar, water, and syrup. Flavors are added. For example, there are cherry lollipops, apple lollipops, and many more kinds of lollipops. Some are swirled with many different colors and flavors. The mixture starts out soft and then hardens on a stick.

Some people think that the idea of lollipops started when children put tiny hard candy on the tops of their pencils in the 1860s. They would suck on the candy while they were working at school. Experts aren't exactly sure when people started putting hard candy on a stick. They're unsure because many everyday people made this treat at home before it was sold in stores. It's impossible to know when the first person did this. In fact, more than one person probably did it at the same time.

Lollipops weren't made by companies and sold in stores until the early 1900s. Some say that the lollipop was invented by the owner of a candy company. He would put extra candy mixtures on a stick at the end of the day. He took these treats to his children. He eventually started to make and sell the candy on a stick.

Some historians think lollipops are even older. They think they started when cavemen gathered honey with a stick. They think these people might have licked the extra honey off the stick when they finished. This sweet treat could have been the first lollipop!

Today, lollipops come in many different forms. Some have gum in the middle, others are very sour, and some even sizzle in your mouth! You can even find sugar-free suckers if you're trying to be healthy.

The most popular lollipop is probably the all-day lollipop or all-day sucker. You can buy these super-sized sugary treats at some candy stores. They are very popular at circuses, fairs, and carnivals. An all-day lollipop is enormous. Some might even be as big as your head! They're called all-day lollipops because it might take you all day to finish one!

Next time you get an all-day lollipop, see how many hours it takes you to finish. Does it really last an entire day?

Match each word to its antonym. Write the letter on the line. Use the context in the reading to help you.

1. _____ guessing

2. _____ hard

3. _____ on

4. _____ different

5. _____ start

6. _____ tiny

7. _____ experts

8. _____ sure

9. _____ sweet

10. _____ sugar-free

a. everyday people

b. sugary

c. finish

d. off

e. exactly

f. sour

g. soft

h. enormous

i. unsure

j. same

The End!

A.

Linda Summers was an ordinary girl until she held a lizard on a trip to Mexico. When she returned home, strange things started happening. First, her skin started to get scaly and dry. She put lotion on it every day, but it didn't help. Then her tongue grew long and slippery. Next, her eyes started to bulge out and move in different directions.
She was turning into a reptile! She noticed she had super-human strength. She was able to leap high, and she could stick her tongue to buildings and swing from them. She also had amazing vision. She called herself Lizard Linda, and she used her powers to fight crime.

One day, she was chasing some bank robbers out of a bank. As she went through the revolving door, her tongue got stuck. She went around and around and couldn't get out.

B.

Dan met Jorge at Six Lakes Summer Camp in 2003. They became great friends. When camp ended, they e-mailed each other every day. They sent each other text messages, too. They never went to the camp again, but they stayed friends for years.

By 2060, technology had improved a lot. They spoke to each other on videophones. They could see each other while they were talking. They held the screen in their hands and had chips in their ears to listen to each other. Dan had a son named Tommy, and Jorge had a son named Carlos. Their children even got to know each other on the videophones.

C.

Nelson Winters hated to wear shoes. He went barefoot wherever he could during the summer. His parents didn't mind if he was barefoot around the house. They didn't mind if he was barefoot at the park. They did mind if he was barefoot when he rode his bike. They told him it was too dangerous because he could hurt his feet. They made him wear shoes on his bike.

The problem was that every time Nelson wanted to ride his bike, he couldn't find his shoes. That's when he thought of an idea. He searched for an hour and finally found his tennis shoes. He strapped them to the handlebars of his bike with heavy rubber bands.

Match each story to a possible ending. Write A, B, or C. Each story has more than one possible ending.

1. Now he never had to look for his shoes when he rode his bike. He just slipped his shoes on and got on the bike. His parents were very happy. _____

2. In 2120, their great-grandchildren talked to each other with hallophones. They could see images of each other in the rooms even though they lived far away. Their grandparents would have been happy to know that they were friends. _____

3. She was spinning so fast that all of her scales fell off. Her eyes turned back to normal. Her tongue did too, and she was unstuck. The police caught the robbers, and she turned back into a normal girl. _____

4. She started pushing the doors faster and faster. Finally the doors broke and she flew out of the bank. She landed right on top of the robbers and saved the day! _____

5. One summer they sent their sons to Six Lakes Summer Camp. Their children met each other in person and became great friends. _____

6. He called his invention the Bicishoe. His neighbor worked for a bike company and liked the idea. Now the Bicishoe is sold all over the world. _____

Circle the best title for each story.

7. Story A
   a. "Linda Summers and Linda Lizard"
   b. "Linda Loves Mexico"
   c. "Linda Uses Lotion"

8. Story B
   a. "Technology in 2060"
   b. "Computers at Summer Camp"
   c. "Summer Camp Leads to a Long Friendship"

9. Story C
   a. "Nelson Winters's Feet Smell"
   b. "Nelson Winters Invents the Bicishoe"
   c. "Nelson Winters's Parents Make Rules"

10. Which story do you like best?

_____

Answer Key

Answers to some pages may vary.

Page 5
1. b
2. a
3. c
4. b
5. c
6. a
7. b
8. a
9. a
10. c

Page 7
1. false
2. true
3. true
4. false
5. true
6. false
7. true
8. false
9. false
10. false

Page 9
1. the control panel
2. to the International Space Station
3. a space suit and space food
4. Mars
5. Robo's paw prints
6. because it's made of gas
7. a few pieces of space dog food
8. a space ball
9. rocketed to and head to
10. desolate

Page 11
1. be
2. teenagers
3. interest
4. separate
5. made
6. remember
7. money
8. costs
9. protect
10. put

Page 13
1. b
2. c
3. a

4. c
5. a
6. b
7. a
8. c
9. b
10. c

Page 15
6 Deedee turns eight.
12 Deedee's friend gives her a lamp with a doll on it.
4 Deedee gets a mug with her name on it.
13 Deedee turns twelve.
7 Deedee decides to collect key chains.
14 Deedee's parents buy her a doll with a dog.
5 Deedee starts to collect things with her name on them.
1 Deedee starts to collect dogs.
9 Deedee starts collecting stones.
2 Deedee celebrates her sixth birthday.
11 Deedee collects lamps.
3 Deedee starts to collect mugs.
8 Deedee's brother gives her a key chain with a stone on it.
10 Deedee celebrates her tenth birthday.

Page 17
1. St. Petersburg, Russia
2. Berlin, Wisconsin
3. St. Petersburg, Russia; Paris, France; Berlin, Germany
4. Dublin, Ohio
5. San José, Costa Rica; St. Petersburg, Russia; Panama City, Panama
6. Paris, Texas
7. Paris, France
8. Panama City, San José
9. Dublin, Ohio
10. St. Petersburg, Florida; St. Pete

Page 19
1. window
2. tower
3. gate
4. wall
5. moat

6. drawbridge
7. true
8. false
9. true
10. false

Page 21
1. give up
2. go up
3. climb up
4. pull up
5. hang up
6. pick up
7. come up
8. bring up
9. clean up
10. fix up

Page 23
1. b
2. a
3. b
4. a
5. c
6. c
7. b
8. a
9. b
10. c

Page 25
1. download; technology
2. hamburger; another language
3. barrio; another language
4. chill out; slang
5. Blackberry; technology
6. monitor; technology
7. cool; slang
8. dude; slang
9. feng shui; another language
10. e-mailed; technology

Page 27
1. Olivia
2. because the string broke
3. because it was too dark to see
4. Oliver
5. They wrote postcards.
6. Oliver
7. Oliver's brother
8. frustrated
9. humorous
10. Oliver and Olivia's parents, friends, a teacher

Page 29
1. pins
2. lane
3. bowling ball
4. bowling shoes
5. spare
6. strike
7. scorecard
8. true
9. false
10. true

Page 31
1. f
2. c
3. a
4. g
5. i
6. b
7. e
8. j
9. d
10. h

Page 33
1. c
2. a
3. c
4. b
5. a
6. a
7. b
8. c
9. a
10. c

Page 35
1. inference
2. fact
3. fact
4. inference
5. fact
6. inference
7. inference
8. fact
9. fact
10. inference

Page 37

ADOPT	a pet, a whale, a tree, a highway
CLEAN	a highway, a park
VOLUNTEER	your time, at a nursing fac...
DONATE	clothes, books, money, t...
PLANT	a tree, flowers

Page 39

Paula	kind, creative
Perry	fluffy, frisky
Prince	cute, cuddly
Penelope	furry, friendly
Paula's parents	frustrated, understanding
"Penny"	small, silky

Page 41
1. d
2. h
3. f
4. c
5. a
6. j
7. e
8. i
9. b
10. g

Page 43
1. c
2. b
3. b
4. a
5. b
6. c
7. c
8. b
9. a
10. b

Page 45
9 Farah gave her parents gold jewelry.
6 Fabian saw two goblins.
3 Franklin found a fairy.
12 Fabian threw gold dust at the party.
2 The children went into the forest.
4 The fairy led Franklin to a cave with a treasure chest in it.
11 The King and Queen had a party.
5 An elf took Farah to treasure buried in the ground.
10 Fabian told his parents friendship is the best treasure in the world.
8 Franklin gave his parents gold coins.
1 The King and Queen asked their children to find treasures.
7 The goblins told Fabian friendship is the best treasure in the world.

Page 47
1. c, f

2. a, d
3. b, i
4. g, k
5. e, h

Page 49
1. between $\frac{1}{2}$ and $1\frac{1}{2}$ inches
2. small creatures
3. 1–5 years
4. 34
5. d
6. f
7. a
8. c
9. e
10. b

Page 51
1. a
2. c
3. a
4. b
5. a
6. b
7. b
8. c
9. a
10. c

Page 53
1. no information
2. true
3. false
4. true
5. false
6. true
7. no information
8. false
9. true
10. no information

Page 55
1. soda and ice cream
2. in the 1950s
3. fruit juice and chunks of real fruit
4. in the 1990s
5. options
6. chocolate
7. gummy bears and sprinkles
8. an ice cream sundae
9. more than one flavor
10. fad

Page 57
1. Isabel
2. Victoria
3. Victoria
4. Isabel
5. Victoria
6. Victoria
7. Isabel
8. Isabel, Victoria
9. Isabel

10. Isabel, Victoria

Page 59
1. b
2. a
3. a
4. c
5. c
6. b
7. b
8. a
9. c
10. a

Page 61
1. 6.5 feet
2. 8 feet
3. 450-550 pounds
4. horse, zebra, giraffe
5. leaves, grass, and fruit
6. leopards
7. b
8. c
9. a
10. d

Page 63
1. joey
2. Outback
3. vegetarian
4. Joey
5. vegetarian
6. pouch
7. crocodile
8. Outback
9. pouch
10. crocodile

Page 65
1. car
2. metal
3. Russia
4. Paris
5. 50
6. coal
7. 1930s
8. different
9. amuse
10. roller coasters

Page 67
1. g
2. b
3. i
4. e
5. f
6. c
7. d
8. a
9. j
10. h

Page 69
7 Doug, Dorothy, Grandma,

and Grandpa sit down and eat ice cream.
2 Grandpa drives to the amusement park.
10 Dorothy and Doug tell their parents about their amusing day.
6 A woman makes sure Dorothy is tall enough to ride the carousel.
9 Grandpa and Grandma take Dorothy and Doug home.
1 Donut hides in the backseat of Grandma and Grandpa's car.
5 Everyone claps when *Iguanas on Ice* ends.
3 Grandma and Doug scream on the *Speedy Bullet*.
8 Grandpa points to a sign that says *Pet Palace*.
4 Grandpa and Grandma help someone with directions while Doug and Dorothy are in the *Mad Castle*.

Page 71
1. opinion, visit
2. fact, fifth
3. fact, plane
4. opinion, money
5. fact, surprised
6. opinion, Cappuccino
7. fact, museums
8. opinion, play
9. opinion, country
10. fact, New York City

Page 73
1. true
2. false
3. true
4. false
5. true
6. false
7. true
8. true
9. false
10. true

Page 75
1. c
2. b
3. a
4. c
5. c
6. b
7. a
8. c
9. b
10. c

Page 77
1. b
2. c
3. c
4. a
5. b
6. c
7. a
8. b
9. b
10. b

Page 79
1. transportation
2. competition
3. recreation
4. exercise
5. collection
6. art
7. work
8. transportation
9. competition
10. work

Page 81
1. Dan
2. Carla
3. Lekisha
4. Dan
5. Dan, Carla
6. Lekisha
7. Mario
8. Dan, Mario, Lekisha, Carla
9. Dan, Mario, Lekisha, Carla
10. Mario

Page 83
1541 An explorer gets to the Mississippi.
1828 The founder of the Red Cross is born.
1884 The 33rd president of the US is born.
1886 Coca-Cola is invented.
1902 A volcano erupts and kills many people.
1919 The first moment of silence is held.
1933 Gandhi stops eating to protest.
1933 Radios are put in police cars.
1950 Floods kill people in Nebraska.
1973 The argument at Wounded Knee ends.
1975 Enrique Iglesias is born.
1999 A woman graduated from the Citadel.

Page 85
1. h
2. e
3. b

4. j
5. f
6. d
7. g
8. a
9. i
10. c

Page 87
1. c
2. a
3. c
4. b
5. c
6. b
7. a
8. b
9. c
10. c

Page 89
1. Hollywood Ending
2. Surprise Ending
3. Cliffhanger
4. judge
5. edge
6. solve
7. expecting
8. reunited
9. spoil
10. reveal

Page 91
1. e
2. g
3. d
4. j
5. c
6. h
7. a
8. i
9. f
10. b

Page 93
1. C
2. B
3. A
4. A
5. B
6. C
7. a
8. c
9. b
10. Answers may vary.